PRAISE *for Mary T. Wagner*

"A pleasure to read. I'm convinced Mary T. Wagner is the reincarnation of Erma Bombeck...in sexier shoes."

JOHN DeDAKIS, *author of "Fast Track," "Bluff" and "Troubled Water"*

"Mary's writing is honest, which is the best thing I think writing can be. Her humor, sincerity and attention to detail make her a writer for anyone in need of a good story. Heartfelt and witty, her pieces move to the beat of a woman-who-knows marching in stilettos. Brilliant!"

ALYSON LYON, *co-founder of Chicago's Essay Fiesta*

"These wonderful stories are not just observations about women, they're about all of us."

DAVID W. BERNER, *author, "Any Road Will Take You There"*

"Mary's stories are thought provoking and entertaining. You feel the life in her words as you're reading them."

GRACIE HILL, *author, "Where the Brothers At?" and "Sorrows of the Heart"*

"Mary Wagner has an artist's eye for detail, a keen sense of what is meaningful in life, and an unerring ability to capture it all in wonderfully readable prose. No woman who loves or works or dreams or simply lives in the world today will fail to find something with which to connect.

CYNTHIA CLAMPITT, *author, "Waltzing Australia"*

ALSO BY MARY T. WAGNER

Running with Stilettos

Heck on Heels

Fabulous in Flats

WHEN THE SHOE FITS...

Essays of Love, Life and Second Chances

♦ ♦ ♦ ♦

By Mary T. Wagner

WATERHORSE PRESS

WHEN THE SHOE FITS...

Essays of Love, Life and Second Chances

First edition August 1, 2014

ISBN-13: 978-0615991740
ISBN-10:   0615991742

*Cover photos by the author at the **Museum of Wisconsin Art***

Visit the author's website at
www.marytwagner.com

WATERHORSE PRESS

Contents

This book is dedicated to my grandson Kai...
on whom the sun rises and sets!

Nana,

It was lovely to meet you
in Wisconsin Rapids!
Work + art = a winning
combination.

all the best,

Mary T. Wagner

Forward

I was standing in my bare feet on the polished stone floor of the second floor lobby in the courthouse where I work as a prosecuting attorney. The cold seeped into my toes as I clasped my no-nonsense spike heels in one hand. Framed by walls of polished, pink Georgia marble shot through with veins of silver and black, a couple of other courtroom staffers and I stood in an alcove a few feet from the courtroom door. Just moments earlier, a sheriff's deputy had rushed into the room, gun drawn, searching for an escaping felon.

Not finding his quarry, the uniformed officer ushered us quickly out of the courtroom for safekeeping. Just a few minutes prior to that, all of us in the courtroom had been startled by the scuffling sounds of someone running on the floor above us. Then the judge caught a glimpse of someone dashing through his chambers which were situated off to the side of the courtroom and away from view of the public. And then as we wondered what was going on, the deputy ran in.

The sounds of pursuit still rang and echoed through the building and around our little knot in the lobby, and we wondered what would happen next. And that's when I decided to discretely slip out of my brown spectator pumps with the three-inch stacked heels. I figured that in the very near future, I might either have to run really fast...or I might just have to hurt somebody.

So go the occasional mental meanderings of a woman wearing dangerous shoes.

In the end, the felon escaped from the courthouse, and we all went back to our routines. We learned later that he had dashed into a waiting car, ditched his unwitting accomplice just a few blocks away, and then led police on a chase that ended when he crashed the car and injured himself badly on a highway miles from where he started.

Once it was clear that he had flown the coop, so to speak, life and routine picked up apace on what otherwise had been a routine work day. In other words, I put my high heels back on.

I was a late-bloomer when it comes to high heels, just as I was a late bloomer when it came to becoming a lawyer. But I've learned to enjoy the shoes for such diverse reasons as style (well, what woman doesn't like that?), added height (always a great equalizer in a largely male-dominated courtroom environment), and the fact that I often think of them as "weaponized shoes." In pink, black patent, and of course, indigo faux snakeskin. Seriously, if you're not packing a gun or a taser, you might as well ponder the self-defense possibilities in your wardrobe.

2

With all due respect to Forrest Gump and his mama, Forrest really got it completely wrong. Life is **not at all** like a box of chocolates. At least not for women. Life is more like a shoe store. A really, really **big** store with eternal variety within its walls, and all of the shoes in your size. Yes, of course that part is total fantasy. But then so was Forrest Gump.

I think about shoes a lot these days. Most of the time, I'm just trying to figure out what heels go with what dress or jacket before I leave for work. Black patent? Butter yellow? Burgundy suede? I could still be overcompensating for the fact that I never bought a pair of spike heels until I was past forty. My first book, in fact, and the blog that started it all, was called "Running with Stilettos" and the cover featured a pair of my spike heels on the beach.

A therapist could, I'm sure, read many layers of nuance into that paragraph and that cover image, and bill me for a year or two of sessions on the couch. Been there, done that in sporadic fashion, with "aha" moments and weepy revelations like knots in a rope marking fathoms for the Ancient Mariner.

I view the evolution of shoes in my closet much the same way as a shrink might. But it's a **lot** cheaper and far more entertaining than therapy. I see that my past still claims me, since I retain a fondness for running shoes, regardless of whether I travel faster than a brisk walk these days. I still hold on to a pair of leather riding boots for the rare occasion I may find myself back on a horse.

But the sensible low-heeled pumps that passed for "dress-up" when I was a soccer mom driving a car pool have given way to spike heels of a much sleeker ilk. Most of my "sensible" low-heeled shoes have been tossed. In their place stand a pair of black leather motorcycle boots, which represent an entire evolutionary chapter of their own.

Then there are the lace-up brown leather work boots I wear when I'm out trimming brush with my cordless chain saw. And my snowshoes work best when I wear a pair of shearling-lined paddock boots I splurged on a few years ago. I have trod the time-worn stones of the Appian Way in Mary Jane flats with cushy, crenelated soles faintly resembling small tugboats, and argued the only case I ever *lost* before the state supreme court in the same stilettos that graced my first book cover. The adventure—in shoes and in life—continues.

So when the shoe fits...

Buy it. Really, you even have to ask? Invest in your life, in your style, in your self-confidence, in your best sense of yourself. Claim that beckoning pair as an extension of you. Give yourself permission to say "this feels right." If your "inner voice" is speaking to you, then *start listening to it!!* If you've been turning a deaf ear to it before this, it's about damned time.

Wear it. Don't be a shrinking violet. Embrace the decision you've made and then build on it.

Repair it. The best things in life may be free, but that doesn't mean they don't take some maintenance. Relationships, houses, friendships, love, health, sanity...none of them thrive on neglect or indifference. And sometimes, when they break down, it takes just a little work to set things right again.

Keep looking. Just because it fits and seems comfortable at this exact moment doesn't mean that you can't do better...or push yourself harder.

Buy it in more than one color. When something feels sublimely, perfectly right...why restrict yourself to a narrow set of choices? Integrate what feels marvelous into every corner of your life. Quit compartmentalizing. It didn't do Bill Clinton any good.

Discard it. It can sometimes take a really, really long time to realize that something that is so familiar to you and woven into the fabric of your life can be doing you more damage that it's worth. That holds true for shoes, relationships, jobs, places, habits. There is no shame in finally waking up and changing your mind.

Share it. Where would we be without each other? I wouldn't have bought my first pair of gorgeous, empowering spike heels if my daughter hadn't been standing beside me, encouraging me to take the risk. Whether you have a pair of "magic shoes" or "magic words" at your disposal, share the joy. Share the encouragement. Share the wisdom. Share the fun. And if you have something good to say to someone, say it sooner rather than later. It can sometimes make more of a difference than either of you can imagine.

Conquer your world in it. Be brave and daring in your choices, and always put your best foot forward! Whether you're stepping into a courtroom, a new job, a marathon, or the first day of a walking routine to try to lose some extra weight, turn your face to the sun and the wind, and step bravely into it.

Fortune favors the bold, in footwear and much else. And it's never too late to realize that…and then put your favorite shoes on and do something about it.

Chain Reaction

You can look at it finally abandoning the last of the feminine "rescue" fantasies. Or maybe it was just a dose of latent pioneer spirit finally coming to the surface. Though Davy Crockett never had one of these. (Of course, Davy Crockett never had a pair of leopard-print stilettos in his closet either. Or so we hope.)

Either way, I bought a chain saw.

My favorite dead tree had come down in a thunderstorm that swept through with brief and sudden fury while I stood in the video section of the grocery store looking for a copy of the chick flick, "Ever After." Not getting drenched as I dashed to the car—or swept off to Oz—was the only thing on my mind as I made a run for it through the sheets of water flying sideways through the parking lot and headed for home.

Then I rounded the last of the curve in the driveway, and hit the brakes. High beams illuminated a swath of dead wood spread across the concrete, making the last fifty feet to the garage impassable. Bark and branches were scattered everywhere, and the trunk was split and broken into huge chunks. I'd have my work cut out for me the next morning. I drove my itty-bitty Honda delicately around the carnage and on to the strip of grass next to the flower beds, and put the car away. I fell asleep pondering my options.

As dead trees stood, I hated to see this one go. It had expired several years earlier from unknown causes, along with a dozen or more in the same stretch of the front acres. I had spent the last few winters wondering just when this one would either fall on one of the cars, or just drop across the driveway moments before someone left for work or school. But where most visitors surveyed its precarious placement and said "that's gotta come down before it falls on something," I looked at it and wistfully countered, "maybe another year?"

Perched just feet from the edge of the driveway, this tree had provided more amusement dead than alive. Woodpeckers had drilled holes in the trunk, and they nested there the previous summer. I found this out when I went searching for the source of incredible chattering that occurred nearby in the mornings while I was trying to catch a little more sleep. Living out in the country, the birds are never silent in the morning. But this took nature's alarm clock to a whole new level.

Process of elimination finally led me to the dead tree, and I stationed myself in front of it and waited. And waited. Minutes passed, and nothing happened. And then there was movement in the shadow of one of the nest holes. A fluffy black-and-white head with a pointy beak popped up long enough to get a bead on me, then vanished again. It was a nest of downy woodpeckers, for years frequent visitors to my feeder. Catching a glimpse of them in the hole-ridden snag became a daily game for me, sort of a "Wild America" version of the arcade game "whack-a-mole." But now the next set of nesting woodpeckers would just have to live elsewhere.

The tree had shattered when it hit the pavement, and I separated most of the giant tangle of wood and bark by simply finding the fracture lines, then snapping the branches in the other direction. A pile of dead wood grew in the back yard, promising a blaze of glory like a Viking funeral pyre when lit. The driveway slowly cleared, but huge twisted branches and shattered trunks still lay across the lawn, like naked corpses waiting for burial.

Hmmmmm....what to do? Wait a week or two for my boyfriend to finish his own voluminous yard work and finally bring out his chain saw to make me some firewood? Break out my hand saw and try to do it the old fashioned way? My shoulders and neck still ached from the rudimentary clean-up job I had already done. It might finally be time to go shopping.

I had been in this position once before, a couple of years earlier. Stumbling across fallen branches on a snowy footpath in the dark one evening to admire the deer my son had just brought down nearby, I knew that snowshoeing would be a deathtrap if I didn't clear the trail soon. I took myself to Menards the next morning, and reluctantly perused the chain saw section.

They all looked big. They all looked dangerous. They all looked heavy, and menacing, and manly, and hard to handle. They looked like an invitation to gasoline-powered amputation. I

9

furrowed my brow and paced back and forth. "Can I help you, ma'am?" A polite young man in a blue apron stood ready to assist. I wasn't going to be easy to please.

"Do you have anything smaller?" I asked, already sensing the answer. Did these come in anything like a "Lady Remington" version? Something stamped SAFETY all over, suitable for the Sesame Street set? Something that could guarantee that I wouldn't cut off my own foot? Something specifically built for the female customer…and for good measure, did it come in a different color scheme?

"Maybe you'd be more comfortable with a hand saw," he suggested, and that's what I eventually walked out with. The hand saw worked just fine—and gave my back and arms a good workout to boot—for just about every woodcutting project I had until this one.

I made my way back to Menards. I stopped at Starbucks first on this glorious and sunny day for a mocha Frappuccino. A girl's got to start the day right…and caffeine gives you courage. I walked through the front door of the store with no more enthusiasm than I'd had the last time. Even less, in fact. I'd **seen** that episode of "CSI" where the bloody homicide is eventually solved by the revelation that some idiot didn't know how to handle his own chain saw and had killed himself by accident.

I found the death and dismemberment row…er, the chain saw section. I slowly made my way down the aisle once more, this time noting that the main distinguishing feature of all these was that some were powered by small gasoline motors (the smell!), and others operated with an electric cord. Yes, I could foresee much disaster from tripping over a chain saw cord the same way you trip over the cord to the living room lamp.

And then I saw it. I had nearly overlooked it in my gloom, and in the shadows cast by its larger cousins. Sitting at eye level but with its chain facing away from me, like a puppy burrowed into a pile of blankets, was...the answer to my dilemma. It was a tiny, battery-operated chain saw. I stared in amazement. The thing was tiny, weighing barely six pounds. I picked it up. I have kitchen appliances that are bigger. It was rechargeable. The "bar" was only eight inches long. It looked like two bigger chain saws had had a baby. My breadmaker came in a bigger box. Despite the color scheme—a utilitarian, no, let's be honest, perfectly ugly—black and orange, it was actually *cute*.

It seemed like a perfect fit. I bought it, of course, and learned to use it. I like being rescued just as much as the next girl. But I confess that my favorite scene in "Ever After" comes at the very end when Drew Barrymore—the beleaguered Cinderella of the story—manages to turn the tables on her lecherous captor and frees herself at sword point. It catches her handsome prince a bit by surprise when he gallantly shows up late for the rescue, but he gets over it. And then some.

Back in the present day and "the real world," I confess to a joy and satisfaction that is absolutely *primordial* when I feed some of the wood that I've cut into the fireplace to warm my living room, or add it to the "burn pile" outside to keep a bonfire going. Yes, I buy most of my firewood elsewhere, and have it delivered straight to the wood rack in my garage.

But I can still recognize my own handiwork in that motley assortment. And I feel a lovely sense of empowerment every time I take my little chain saw out to do some yard work or clear another fallen tree that's blocked the driveway.

Now…if only it came in pink!

Turbo Dating—A Year in Review

I am really tired of reading "bad date" stories. It seems like every women's magazine, every newspaper, every trendy "lifestyle" website has an article about memorably awful encounters, particularly for single women over thirty-five. Moaning artfully about meeting Mr. Wrong has turned into a cottage industry.

The stories themselves are uniformly arch, and funny, and full of razor-sharp detail, from the gleam on the rim of a martini glass in flickering candlelight to the click of a date's false teeth, and the barely concealed look of disappointment on a middle-aged guy who had hoped to meet someone younger. The women in these modern dating chronicles are witty, plucky, resilient and cheerfully determined. And the tales are grounded in incompatibility and disappointment. If fairy tales end naturally in happy unions, these wickedly downbeat and sardonic narratives thrive on skepticism and dissatisfaction.

Here's a different perspective, based on what I now call my "Year of Turbo Dating." This was the year of catching up I embarked on after my twenty-plus year marriage ended. In the final

13

tally, I drank a lot of coffee, made a lot of small talk, had some bad dates, had some great dates, met some fellas who didn't make it past the "sixty second rule" and met some guys who were really wonderful.

But at the end of that action-packed twelve months—including "meet 'n' greets" with three dozen guys—I had learned that the best and most important relationship I found was with myself.

The turbo dating year kicked off, naturally, with a divorce. I had pulled the plug on a twenty-five year marriage a month before the actual anniversary. The marriage had been on life-support for a decade before that. While the general public was surprised, our children were not.

At the age of barely twenty-four, with no dating experience to speak of behind me, I had married my first steady boyfriend. We met as he was finishing law school and I was finishing up a degree in journalism. Four children soon followed, and I immersed myself in full-time motherhood, with a career as a freelance magazine writer on the side.

Fifteen years later a horseback riding accident put me in a body cast for three months, and I suddenly looked at life in a very new way. Law school followed, then a career as a criminal prosecutor, and eventually the bonds of matrimony cracked and broke. Seven months later, after a civilized "collaborative divorce," I was suddenly single.

The general rule of thumb, or so I've been told, is that the newly divorced should give themselves a couple of years to heal their emotional wounds before jumping into the dating pool. I, on the other hand, have always been something of a loose cannon, and so I waited all of four days after the ink was dry on the divorce decree before I signed up to try on-line dating. It was only a few hours before someone hit on my profile and tentatively suggested getting together.

I couldn't have predicted my reaction. At that instant I recoiled from the keyboard as if it was on fire, realizing that I was *soooooooo* not ready for this!! But a few weeks later, I finally took the plunge and scheduled two coffee dates for a weekend. In for a dime, in for a dollar.

Bachelor Number One turned out to be a walking object lesson for the fact that you can't tell what someone actually looks like in a single "long shot" photo. And that well-written emails can mask the fact that English may only be your second language. I am still not sure what his first language was…but we still spent an hour chatting with difficulty above the noise in a crowded coffee shop.

I patted him genially on the shoulder as we parted company and said "I'm sure the right girl is out there for you!" Then I walked swiftly away…but not before he'd regaled me with tales of his own internet dating horror stories. He also left me with a piece of advice which I still consider priceless. That you can talk all you want about compatibility points and shared interests and matching core values...but what it really still all comes down to is

15

"chemistry." How you answer the question, "do you want to get closer to this person?" I put that thought in the back of my mind and set out to meet Bachelor Number Two.

This turned out to be a good looking, articulate accountant who owned a sailboat. My passion for my work as a prosecutor appeared to captivate him, and an hour of animated conversation flew by. He asked me out again, this time to dinner at a romantic lakefront restaurant. He cleaned up quite nicely. So did I. Drinks, dinner, dress-up clothes instead of my usual jeans and sweats, a little canoodling in the parking lot before parting...I couldn't have asked for a better first "real date" to start me off.

A third date, at an art museum, was calendared in. And halfway through it I had one of those "eureka moments" that cartoonists illustrate with light bulbs floating overhead. I realized we didn't get excited about any of the same stuff. And worse, I was dialing down most of my enthusiasm to match his cynicism and malaise. It was the wrong way to go. I think he felt it too. We exchanged a brisk hug and a peck in the museum parking lot, and then we both drove away and never looked back. The adventure continued, and so did the education of Mary.

I kept my dating life under the radar from my children for a very long time, but regaled my girlfriends at work with tales from the front. And the theme that always floated to the top was that with every conversation, with every meeting, with every disappointment or pleasant surprise, I came away knowing a little more about myself.

I was finally getting to ask myself the questions I would have asked at the age of twenty if I had possessed a social life back then. Preconceptions went right out the window as my coffee intake increased. ***Well I thought I liked that***…but maybe not as much as I expected. ***Gee, didn't know I liked that in a man!*** Who knew? ***Hmmm…I guess I don't really like that after all***.

And so it went.

Even the few memorably bad experiences taught me something. Such as the fact that it's okay to be impatient and even downright aggravated.

One evening found me in a trendy restaurant sharing drinks and appetizers with a good looking guy who had even described himself that night as an "angry white male." After his first lengthy rant—about the press and its "contempt for the military"—I found myself wondering if I would have the guts to slap a twenty on the counter and just walk out. I didn't, and an excruciating evening ground on until his second rant—this time about illegal immigration—ran its course. As I drove home forty miles in the dark, I thought ruefully, "I skipped sitting home in my pajamas and watching **'Medium'** for this??" Next time, I vowed, I would be quicker to leave and cut my losses.

And then there were the kinder, gentler encounters. A guy who showed up nervously with flowers to meet me for the first time. He revealed that it was his first date in the year that had followed his divorce, and he was scared to death to start testing the waters.

17

There was the blue-collar guy who drove a cement truck most of the year, and a snow plow in the winter months. He was cute and funny and wore a diamond earring, and while we didn't technically call all the hanging out that we did actual "dating," we laughed and talked about life and politics for months, did stuff, flew a kite into a tree, met for dinner when I was passing by. For a long time he was my "go to" guy for answers to all the manly questions I knew nothing about, such as how to use my new cordless drill and how to maintain the water heater. I told him that in a blizzard, given a choice between Brad Pitt coming up the driveway on a white horse with a dozen roses and the guy with a snowplow, every woman I know would pick the guy with the plow, feeling like the cavalry had arrived for a rescue. He liked that image a lot.

Then there was the draftsman who, when I warned him before meeting that some guys found dating a "chick with a badge" a bit scary, showed up for coffee sporting a toy badge of his own pinned to his flannel shirt. I felt charmed right out of my socks.

There was a perfectly wonderful widower in the mix, too. Our emails were great. Our phone conversations were great. The two-hour brunch we shared as a first date was great, and we left the restaurant pleasantly committed to finding time soon for a second. But by the end of the day, we had both agreed to call it off. On the long drive home, I had realized that his two little boys really needed a mother figure in their lives. And after raising four children already, it wasn't going to be me. He, on he other hand, had noticed me unconsciously flinch when he brought out the pictures of his young sons, and realized that some gulfs can't be bridged. And so I learned that sometimes you have to be a grownup right out of the gate, even when it hurts.

I kept to a general rule of not going out with anyone farther away than 75 miles, but even that rule was meant to be broken. After months of charming and intriguing emails and phone conversations with a wildlife artist in another state, we finally agreed to meet half-way and go bird watching. We split the difference at about two hundred miles apiece, and rendezvoused one morning at a wildlife refuge. Officially, we were there to look for whooping cranes. Ha!

He turned out to be a little bit older looking than his picture, but he was still craggily handsome in a self-assured, outdoorsy way. I don't think I passed *his* sixty second rule. But we still spent a glorious day outdoors, enveloped by sunlight and nature, trading stories of life and children and authorities flaunted and obstacles overcome. I'll never forget staring, awestruck, at a quartet of young bald eagles as they playfully soared and swooped together, snatching fish with their talons from the water below and then dive bombing each other to get the others' prize. And at the tail end of the day, after hours of looking, we found an elusive whooping crane, in splendid close-up, after all.

I also found myself irrevocably changed by the evening I spent with a former Navy pilot. He still flew on occasion in his civilian job, but had recently found himself grounded because of high blood pressure. This date was literally a "one night wonder." We talked, we laughed, we teased, we flirted, we ate, we drank…and then we went to a movie so the evening could stretch even longer. We shared volumes about our kids, our lives, our families, our marriages, our disappointments, our joys. And then he called it quits the next day by email. Go figure.

But the encounter had a profound effect on me in a way I could never have predicted. For years I had been a white-knuckle flyer. The older I got, the more afraid I was. Shortly before the pilot and I met, in fact, I had flown to Germany to visit my son who was spending a semester there as a foreign exchange student. And it was only the strength of maternal affection that got me on that plane, terror in my heart and dread in the pit of my stomach.

Now I was in another plane on the tarmac, this time flying to Phoenix to visit a friend from college. And as I sat, again terrified, in my window seat, I made a deliberate choice to try to see the act of flying through that pilot's eyes. Not as something to be endured and steeled against, but as a joy and a release. To trust the technology as proven, to embrace the thrust of liftoff, to see an open horizon as something as inviting and welcoming and liberating as he did.

It worked. Flying hasn't been the same for me since.

After a year of this adventuring, I figured it was finally about time to scale back and take stock. The year had been interesting, but it had been exhausting too. One extraordinary weekend had seen me meet up with four guys in three days…or three guys in four days. Details are fuzzy in a whirlwind. With only four days left on my Match.com membership, I spent a few hours one evening combing through photos and profiles, seeing if there was anyone interesting that I had somehow missed. I came up with a half-dozen possibilities.

Three wrote back. One was a professional sports photographer who was smart, and cute, and so much of a rolling stone we could never agree on a good time to meet. One was "Prince Charming" by email, and was equally charming by telephone. But he just didn't hit the right notes in person.

I decided to break the mold with the third one, and after a flurry of emails and some phone calls, suggested skipping the traditional "coffee date" and meeting instead at a movie theater. He was there on time, and seemed nice and cautiously friendly. We got our popcorn and sodas, settled into our seats, and waited for the commercials to end.

As the start of the movie approached, I turned to him and announced that now was as good a time as any to fess up to the couple of little white lies I had told in my online dating profile. He looked at me with a skeptical squint.

First, I confessed, I wasn't 48 as I'd claimed in my profile, but in fact was 50. He looked straight ahead again and nodded, then asked "and what's the other?"

"Well," I replied, "I'm not slender either."

In profile, I could see the steady, somber features of his face instantly split wide open with a grin and he started to laugh. And as the lights dimmed and the opening credits came on, I settled comfortably back in my velvet seat and smiled, thinking, "I've got a really good feeling about this!"

I still do.

The Limoncello Diaries

This is a tragic story of a bottle of lemon liqueur.

It is also an Italian story of love and loss, romance, hope and dashed expectations, creative splendor and artistry denied, and the totally nutty times we live in.

This saga began with me spending a sunny day on the Isle of Capri in the Bay of Naples. I was in Italy for a whirlwind six-day "guided tour" vacation, a desperately needed break from the past few years of serial family emergencies and other deadlines. The early October sun was warm on my bare shoulders, and my brain was fully in vacation mode, half a planet and a thousand miles away from daily details. And, in the words of one of my favorite Mary Chapin Carpenter songs, I also "don't speak a word of Italian."

But the bottle of Limoncello's story starts even before that, with a bunch of ripe lemons grown under Mediterranean skies in soil rich with volcanic ash, and laboriously processed and aged with sugar and alcohol to produce a sweet liqueur that, along with gelato, is the essence of Italy distilled to dessert. Tiramisu can't hold a candle to those two.

During the preceding several days, I had seen no end of souvenir bottles of Limoncello on display in Rome and Pompeii and Sorrento, many of them shaped like a three-dimensional version of the Italian peninsula. They were garish and clunky, and sparked no desire in me as I indulged my shopping impulses among fine chocolates and a leather shop on a cobblestoned street in Sorrento.

But at the tail end of a day on Capri that included a visit to the famous Blue Grotto, I became enamored of the idea of bringing home a bottle of Limoncello (which in fact originated in Capri) to share with the man in my life who would be waiting for me at the airport. While I had other souvenirs for him tucked away in my suitcase, the idea of celebrating my return with a palpable taste of Italy was rapidly becoming irresistible. He had lived in Italy for several years a long time ago when he was in the military, and his house is decorated with many reminders of that time.

My eye was caught by a display of "Limoncello di Capri" bottles in a shop near the Marina Piccola. They were tasteful. They were attractive. Even empty, I could see keeping the bottle as a flower vase. And they were even packaged in boxes, providing a little extra padding for the long trip home.

I bought one, imagining the smile on my man's face when I brought it out of my tote bag, and hurried to stay close to the tour guide. The bottle of Limoncello and I then crossed the Bay of Naples by high speed ferry to Napoli, where I then transferred to another bus for the three-hour return trip to Rome.

On the day I finally departed, I awoke before daybreak. I took my last shower in my lovely Italian hotel room, then snuck out to the hotel's rooftop garden with a cup of hot "cioccolato" to watch dawn break over the Roman horizon. It was beautiful.

Back in my room, I stuffed the neck of the box with a few pair of underwear to keep the bottle from jiggling, and then carefully wrapped the box in two dresses before tucking it into the bottom of my tote bag. I felt I didn't dare pack it in my soft-sided suitcase for fear the bottle would break. Then, all packed up and with a smile on my face, I checked out of the hotel and waited for my private car transport to the airport. I knew that by the end of the day and the seventeen-hour journey, I would be too tired to open my suitcase, but I looked forward to pouring us a drink and putting my feet up and toasting to a great many things.

I checked my suitcase at the airport, and then trundled off to the security checkpoint. I expected no holdups, since I'd packed all my little bottles of shampoo and moisturizer in the suitcase rather than my carry-on bags. My brain was still clearly in "vacation mode." The thought that all the anti-terrorism precautions requiring us to pack our tiny travel-sized tubes of toothpaste and hair conditioner in quart-sized Ziploc bags for individual scrutiny by the federales would somehow *also* apply to my carrying a bottle of quintessentially Italian booze bought on a whim on a sunny day at a tourist shop never crossed my mind. Just a few years earlier, I had flown home from Germany with two bottles of wine swaddled in bubble wrap and nestled in a backpack which I had carried on to the plane and stored above my seat without a hitch.

I blithely sailed through the metal detector, gathered my purse and tote bag, and headed into the airport. Behind me, someone said "Madame, just a moment." I paid the voice no heed the first and second time, but on the third I finally turned around.

"Who, me?" A female security guard beckoned me back and asked me to put my bags on the table. She said something about the bottle. I dutifully dug out the Limoncello and unwrapped it. I could not bring a bottle of liquid on the plane, she explained politely. My face fell. My options were to either arrange to mail the bottle home, or to throw it away, she said.

"I don't know how to send it," I replied. Was there no one else I was traveling with that could do this for me, she asked. No, I was traveling alone, with no one to hand the task off to.

I shrugged sadly, still in shock. Sometimes you just can't fight City Hall. I opened the top of the box and retrieved my underwear—thank goodness I had packed the neck of the bottle with animal print undies for visual interest in case the security checkpoint inspection would be particularly thorough. It would be one thing to have your bags searched down to the lining by a security detail in Rome, but entirely another to stand accused in this fashionable international capitol of having boring panties.

I reluctantly handed the officer the bottle. "Enjoy," I said with resignation, and we parted company.

I hope, at least, that she or some other officer actually got to take it home and drink it. The thought that this exquisite, lovingly crafted bottle of lemon liqueur would end up in a trash bin at an airport named for Leonardo da Vinci would be just too harsh and ironic to contemplate.

I mentally recalibrated my opening words to the man who would meet me that night, and adjusted them to start with "honey, I bought this great bottle of Limoncello for us in Capri but…" I know it's the thought that counts, but sharing the drink after the journey would have somehow counted for more.

In the meantime, somebody please call Dan Brown for me, I think I have the name of his next book here.

How about "The Limoncello Code"?

Of Shoes and Strategy

They were "death on a staircase" shoes, and they stopped me dead in my tracks.

Sleek leopard print brocade, with pointy toes, squared-off vamps, delicate sling backs, and spike heels that added a good three and a half inches to my height, these were *definitely* trophy shoes.

I tried them on, but the questions I purported to be seriously asking myself as I strode back and forth in the shoe department glancing at the mirror from various angles—could I *really* wear them into a courtroom; what suit and accessories would they *possibly* go with; if I didn't think I'd wear them to work where on *earth* would I ever wear them—were as ritualized and formulaic as Kabuki theater.

Of course I was going to buy them, it was a foregone conclusion. They were gorgeous, and sexy, and the fact I had no place in particular to wear them yet had not deterred me from buying any of their predecessors now sitting in my closet. My working theory that the occasion would follow the shoes was still working just fine, thank you very much. It's a variation on the movie "Field of Dreams." The shoes came home with me.

I bought my first set of stilettos not when I was a lithe and lissome young twenty-something, but when I was…oh, never mind. The fresh-faced and skinny days as a journalism student in college had been lived quite naturally in jeans and sneakers. Marriage and motherhood followed closely on the heels of my graduation and brand-new career as a newspaper reporter. And as every mother knows, rounding up energetic toddlers is a lot like herding cats. You have the best chance of success when you're in running shoes.

Even law school and then a job as a prosecutor didn't reverse the tide. I had already gotten too used to comfort in the interval, conducting transatlantic phone interviews as a freelance writer in my shorts and bare feet and occasionally my pajamas; taking the kids to the beach in flip-flops; racing through the grocery store and leading Brownie troops through adventures in the woods in scuffed Reeboks. Sensible shoes did just fine.

The turning point came, as they usually do, during a time of high stress. One of my children had a mysterious health crisis, and I was killing time between driving her around campus by reading cases in an overstuffed chair by the fireside at Starbucks. Ever the multi-tasker, I was researching drunk driving law for an upcoming argument in court when I had one of those "eureka" moments that Archimedes made famous. Unlike Archimedes, I did not then get up and run wet and naked down the street. I went shoe shopping.

29

For the record, I was looking for some sensible brown shoes. But for some whimsical reason I decided to try on a drop-dead-dangerous pair of faux brown alligator sling-backs with three-inch spike heels. I was timid, and asked the salesperson to put them on hold. I picked my daughter up from class and brought her back to the mall with me. It took her about five seconds to size me up as I teetered in the shoes, and then she delivered a verdict. "Mom, those are really cute. You should buy them." She'd been voted "best dressed" two or three times at her high school. Who was I to argue?

The alligator spikes came home with me and I wore them to work the next day. Another male attorney took one look at them, laughed self-consciously, and said "My God, Mary, those are the sexiest shoes I've ever seen!" It was one of those "light bulb" moments, and I immediately realized that I was on to something.

Spike heels get a bum rap from a lot of quarters. They have been likened to Chinese foot-binding. They have been branded a male conspiracy to keep us helpless and off balance. Described as something that channels the pain of the wearer into the suffering and domination of someone else. An article in National Geographic Magazine, "Every Shoe Tells a Story," quoted British photographer David Bailey as having a fondness for high heels because "[i]t means girls can't run away from me."

If that's what Mr. Bailey really said, I don't think he was grasping the whole picture.

Doesn't anyone remember what Jennifer Jason Leigh's character did to Bridget Fonda's boyfriend with a stiletto heel in the movie "Single White Female"? (*Spoiler alert: he died!*) Or the way Rachel McAdams slowed down a terrorist toward the end of the thriller "Red Eye"? I laughed when I watched her sink her sling-back stiletto into Cillian Murphy's thigh, thinking *I have the same shoes!!* And we've all seen what Jack Bauer is capable of doing with his bare hands week after week in "24." Just imagine what he could do armed with a pair of Manolo Blahniks. Well, okay…maybe we really don't want to go there.

I like to break down some of my own fondness for "limousine shoes" as an exercise in courtroom strategy, since nearly every pair I bring home in a shopping bag finds its way into court with me at some point.

First, there is the height advantage, which is always a good thing in an authority figure. At five-foot-ten in heels, I am easy to spot in a crowd. Then, of course, there's that delightfully authoritative snap of spike heels on a marble floor, an audible warning that indeed, trouble is just around the corner and closing fast. A cop I worked with almost every day for years said he could tell when I was approaching a particular courtroom from behind closed doors just by the rapping of my footsteps in the corridor beyond.

And last—aside from the whole "armed and dangerous" aspect of wearing something that could literally put somebody's eye out—is what I call the "mother-in-law" advantage. It is hard to really pinpoint this, except to say that on some level, if a defendant's mother, or sister, or aunt suddenly stops our group problem-solving discussion to tell me that I've got great shoes, I've gained, well...***something.***

I'm not sure exactly what that is, but it's still something that none of my male colleagues in wing-tips or oxfords will ever experience a glimpse of.

This brings me to one of my favorite stories about just why I keep wearing these death-defying shoes to court, and waiting for the single, aging elevator instead of risking my life on the stairs. One afternoon some time ago, criminal traffic court—involving the traffic violations that can actually land you in jail—was about to start. The defendants' names are usually called in alphabetical order, but sometimes they are called in whatever order a judge feels like just to keep things interesting.

A middle-aged woman came up to me and asked if I could do her a favor by getting her case called early on. Her husband had cancer, she explained, and was home alone. She needed to get back soon to help him with his medications. Was there anything I could possibly do? She was nervous and clearly out of her element in this courtroom, not one of our more regular customers who take their repeat appearances in stride, the "not guilty" plea as reflexive as breathing.

I remember I was wearing a pair of show-stopping plaid stilettos that day, with tiny black patent bows, and I absolutely towered over her in them. She barely came past my chin.

I assured her that I would do what I could, and passed word in advance to the judge that this particular woman could really use a break. We got her in and out of there in a hurry, and she was gracious and effusive in her thanks to all for letting her be on her way quickly under such difficult circumstances.

As she was leaving, she passed me where I was sat at the prosecution table and smiled. Then she caught herself in mid-stride and turned toward me. In front of a room full of defendants, attorneys, courtroom staff and the judge, she breached courtroom decorum, order and dignified routine, stopped, and announced "oh, and I *love* your shoes!!"

The prosecution rests.

Wildflower Seeds and Beer

It started with a handful of small red and white carnations in a glass Coke bottle, propped charmingly and invitingly in the cup holder of a fifteen-year-old navy blue Ford pickup truck. It was February, and it was the dead of winter, and the slush at the curb was up to my ankles when I stepped from the truck to the pavement on the way to an evening of Irish dancing. Flower gardening, never a successful hobby, was the furthest thing on my mind. Staying warm and dry was.

A proper bouquet followed a few days later, and then the next week, a gift of a miniature rose bush with perfect creamy blooms and sturdy green foliage. The rose bush sat on the kitchen counter until the blooms shriveled, and the leaves dropped, and when Spring arrived I finally put it out on the back porch to get some actual sunlight and toughen up. If it was going to live with me, it was going to have to fend for itself.

When it comes to gardening, I freely admit to having a "black thumb." Not black as in fecund, fertile, life-giving soil, Earth Mother, goddess of fertility and all things abundant. Black like the kiss of death. My ability to kill indestructible plants is legendary. Philodendrons. Cactuses. Even Venus Fly Traps. And for heaven's sake, those things are like wild animals, they catch their own prey and feed themselves.

But the man who laid siege to my heart with a tidal wave of thoughtfulness likes to garden. No, that doesn't even do it justice. He is utterly crazy about it. He is always happiest when he's planting some more English daisies or a new variety of columbine. Many things in his yard are watered regularly, and mulched, and tended, and as a result are flourishing. And his garden is forever a work in progress. "Done" is not a word in his vocabulary. Clearly, opposites attract!

The stretch of ground around my house, on the other hand, looked like Death Valley during that first Spring together. I had had some improvements done to the lower level of the house during the previous fall, and all that remained of the few straggly rose bushes that used to snatch at my ankles begging for water, and three huge shrubs, were a handful of ugly stumps and some peony shoots.

We sat on his back porch one warm Spring day, surveying his emerging flower beds, and he explained that he was really, really getting the urge to garden for about the next month. And it was going to either be in his garden, or in mine.

"How about mine?" I suggested. And so the fuse was lit.

My soul began to stir, in small increments at first. I visited a couple of garden centers and bought rose bushes. I purchased a couple of big expensive ones in a spirit of cautious optimism. Mostly, though, I bought plants that cost no more than five bucks. If I was going to kill them, if they were really dead plants walking, I didn't want to spend a lot. I bought a new set of cheap gardening gloves under four dollars. They were sky blue with little pink tulips on the backs. I felt as ready as I'd ever be.

He showed up the next Sunday with the truck loaded with gardening tools, a boom box, a bunch of rock and roll CDs, his teenage daughter, a chain saw and some beer. I weeded and yanked out rotted gardening cloth from beneath mouldering wood chips, served lunch, and pondered where to put the new roses. He chain sawed the stumps to practically nothing, dug out and reset the timbers framing the rose beds to ground level, raked stones out of the dirt and dug the holes for the rose bushes. When the first of the two rose beds were done, we took a break and stood off to the side, admiring the promise of the half-dozen leafless plants we had planted and drenched with water. The dirt was flat and bare, just waiting demurely for a coverlet to look decent.

"So where does a girl go for mulch?" I asked. It was an honest question. Was I supposed to buy it at the garden store by the bag? Order it from a landscape supply place in bulk? Get it delivered by the bushel?

"Oh, I've got that in the back of the truck," he said. **ZING** went the strings of my heart, and I felt my knees go weak. When he left, hours later, my universe had been transformed. Stepping out of my front door, I could see a straight line of rose bushes to the left and right, neatly edged, weed-free, and prettily mulched with shredded cedar. "Oh man, this is like a canvas just waiting to come to life!" he said proudly before he drove off. His enthusiasm was a catchy as a wildfire in a drought.

The next gardening project was far more ambitious. There was stretch of earth beside the house, two hundred feet square and covered by about two-and-a-half tons of gravel with plastic sheeting underneath. After years of weathering, a forest of weeds poked through the plastic. I had looked at it hopelessly, like Sisyphus must have looked up at his mountain after the first few attempts to push that mythical boulder uphill. I knew that with a veritable crew of gardeners and a baron's budget, something could be accomplished, but this was too big a job for one or two people. My muse was not dissuaded. "Man, you could really put a garden in here!" he grinned.

The next Sunday, he offered, we would rendezvous with shovels and his rototiller and start digging, and see how far we got. Hope began to stir cautiously in my heart a little more, one tiny corner at a time. I began to peruse expensive gardening catalogs for plants I thought were pretty, then made almost daily trips to the upscale garden store a mile from my house looking for them priced cheaper in four-inch pots. He brought me a goldfinch feeder and ten pounds of thistle seed to fill it with. I bought a double shepherd's hook to hang the feeder from, and a hanging basket of geraniums to balance it out.

He brought me a watering wand. I hooked a hose up to the spigot by the front door. I bought a few pansies and geraniums to plant around the front of the house, then went searching for some lightweight and artistic pots to put them in. I bought dirt. I bought nemesia, which I'd never heard of before. It's an annual that looks like a mass of tiny orchids, and it looked so appealing that I had to have it, even if I'd have to figure out where to put it later. I bought lavender, and coneflowers, and coreopsis, and three kinds of delphiniums, and coral bells, and evening primroses, and daylilies and phlox. I even bought a butterfly bush. Then six.

I picked my youngest son up from school one day. I was bursting at the seams with pride at finding three tall, matching deep blue delphiniums with white centers at the local garden store. They'd make a nice counterpoint to the butterfly bush, I chattered. I was *so proud!!!* My son looked at me with his eyes glazing over. Still…nothing could rain on my parade!

The gravel-moving project was just as much work as it sounded, but somehow we got it done over the course of two weekends. Plastic was removed, extra rocks raked out, dirt tilled, plants put in and watered. My son helped us to replant phlox and some peonies from a long-abandoned garden attempt while I drove off to buy more mulch. And at some point, during that first day of digging and sweating, an unexpected question was broached.

"Now where would you like a wildflower garden?" *What?* Yes, a genuine wildflower garden could be mine…if I would only pick the spot to be rototilled, and then make a run to the garden store for some wildflower seeds. Oh, and could I please pick up some beer on the way back.

What a shopping list! I dutifully drove while he rototilled. I found some seeds at the garden center, indulged my fancy for another half-dozen perennials in four-inch pots, and brought back a six-pack of Michelob in icy cold glass bottles.

By summer's end, we had finally finished for the year. Although "done" in a gardener's vocabulary is a foreign concept. The perennial plants were all planted, the season for buying annuals had expired, and the wildflowers started to sprout, bursting from the soil a little more every day. We bought a half-ton of Arizona sandstone, drove it home in the pickup truck, sledgehammered it into smaller pavers, and set it into a pretty, staggered footpath through the garden.

In a fit of personal initiative, I even shoveled away more gravel on the other side of the house, ripped out the plastic, broke up the dirt with a shovel, and planted a dozen daylilies...all by myself!

The gardening fever has been catching, along with the joy. For Mother's Day, my son gave me solar powered lanterns to show off the new garden, and a pretty pink mum. I find I spend more time watering plants than I could ever have believed, but it had become a valuable tranquility zone for me. And now that they're being watered once in a while, my rose bushes have never looked so good!

Lest I get too cocky, though, I need look no further than the last part of that Mother's Day gift. My son is thrilled to death with the way the gardens have turned out, and how nice they make the house look when he walks up the drive. He is happy, too, to see me smile as radiantly as I have since this new familiarity with growing things took hold, and the way I blossomed along with the coreopsis and the phlox. But his last word, based on my previous track record, sits carved on a decorative rock in the garden, ready to be moved into position as circumstances and fate should dictate. "I Tried, But It Died," it reads. I hope I don't have to use it very often.

In the meantime, I still have that Coke bottle. And that perfect, miniature rose bush is still growing strong.

Return to the Fatherland

The sleek black Mercedes sedan devoured the autobahn under our tires, purring like a contented panther in high gear as the countryside flew past spotless tinted windows.

"Nicht so schnell!" Not so fast. My father's voice was querulous beside me, a reminder that even if I was driving a car that felt and handled a lot like a jet, I didn't get to push the limits. At least not when he was in the front passenger seat. The speed of the cars passing us in the left lane like the Blue Angels made him nervous, but there was much else to adjust to. For all of us.

My father, myself, and my two teenaged sons were flying along the autobahn in Germany to reunite my dad with the family he had not seen in twenty-five years. Or forty, depending on who in the family you talked to. And we were there because my older son, Michael, had met the German relatives a few months earlier while he was a foreign exchange student, and left a large family gathering absolutely stunned that his grandfather had not seen his sisters in decades.

I had sat with him at the self-same table, understanding not a word of the animated conversation that rapidly swirled around me in German, smiling and nodding and having another glass of wine or slice of cake. I certainly didn't leave the house with the same generous imperative. But from the kindness in his heart and the depth of his conviction that "Mom, I have to fix that!" sprang an odyssey we could never have expected.

Plans were made to take my father and both of the boys to Germany over the Easter school vacation that followed. Cousins and friends overseas were contacted, tickets bought, a car rented, an itinerary roughed out. There was no question that my father deserved the trip. Only months earlier he had remarked that he would love to return to his native Germany before he died. And at eighty-two, especially, nobody is guaranteed another sunrise.

His had not been an easy life for many years. He grew up in a farming village in western Germany, happy there until the start of World War II when he was pressed into service, first as an aircraft mechanic in the Luftwaffe and then, as the war ground on, as a foot soldier. His only brother, Ewald, died on the Russian front with a bullet in his head. He himself surrendered after three days in a foxhole outside Aachen under a barrage of Allied shelling. He spent four years as a prisoner of war, much of it in a coal mine in France. Marriage to my American mother brought him to the United States, and his life here translated into a series of hard and dirty factory jobs in Chicago and Wisconsin to support his family. He never did really grasp the English language very well.

My first inkling that my father's health and his mind were not all that they had been came only four days before we left. I had driven the 120 miles to Chicago with my younger son to get passports issued in person for both of them. Yes, I suppose I could have done this by mail, paid an extra "expedited passport" fee to get them processed quickly. But Hurricane Katrina had wreaked its damage on New Orleans and southern Mississippi not that long before, and my faith in the federal government to accomplish anything in a hurry was at rock bottom.

The three of us went down to the passport office in the Kluczynski Federal Building in Chicago's Loop, and I was shocked by the time we arrived there. Both by how frail my father had become—his skin was like paper and his bones seemed as tiny as a bird's—and how easily confused he was. He possessed not an ounce of stamina, and we cabbed it rather than walk the four blocks to the Art Institute to kill the processing time before the passports would be ready. After a brief lunch, we drove him back home to the city outskirts and then returned to the Loop to pick up the passports later, just to spare him the strain.

Still, there was no thought of calling off the trip. The boys and I gamely tag-teamed him as we traversed the maze of O'Hare Field, airport security, the wait in the lounge to board the plane, and finally our seats on the big Lufthansa jet for our non-stop flight to Frankfurt. Once belted into his seat and aloft, my father relaxed. He had a couple of beers with the boys and a good meal, and chatted animatedly with the lady in the next seat who appeared to find him fascinating.

Ten hours later we landed in Frankfurt in the early morning, retrieved our luggage, picked up the rental car, and began the long drive to my cousin's house. We stopped for coffee and pastry in some small town along the way, walking ever so slowly down the narrow streets and guiding my father away from passing traffic like a child.

Once we arrived at my cousin Ingrid's lovely hilltop home, the festivities were non-stop. My brother and his daughter had come in from Slovenia to join us for a few days, and the entourage grew larger. We spent the afternoon walking through stalls of flower vendors in the village square, and viewed and old castle in Mayen, near Koblenz. We went to evening Mass on Easter Saturday, and drank hot spiced wine afterward around a bonfire by the church.

On Easter Sunday, there was a family reunion at a restaurant in nearby Emmelshausen. As we walked down the street toward the restaurant, my father looking stiffly formal in a navy blazer, an elderly woman and her husband stopped him, dumbfounded.

"Is that you, Willie Wagner?" the woman asked in surprise. The couple hailed from his home town, and had not seen him in half a century. He seemed to recognize the woman, and conversed a little with her in German.

After lunch, we drove, en masse, to the village of Dörth where my father had been born and raised. The church had been restored since the war, and we gazed at the stained glass window dedicated to his fallen brother. Through it all he looked exhausted, and I did not leave his elbow unless there was someone else to take my place. There was a feast later, of course, at my aunt's house.

The family instantly grasped that my father's lucidity was a "sometime" thing, and fussed over him endlessly, an arm draped across his shoulder, a cup of coffee or a glass of wine offered at his elbow. Conversation crackled around him, full of reminiscence and anecdote and affection. Sometimes he stepped right into the talk, a quick stream of German coming from his lips and a spark of connection in his eyes. And then long moments would pass as he sat like a statue, gazing wordlessly into the past. Or at nothing.

The days that followed were filled with joy and activity and excitement. We took a boat trip down the Rhine, followed by another big family dinner. Photo albums were produced, with the question "Willie, do you remember?" Sometimes he spoke, sometimes he nodded, sometimes he just said nothing. There were times he spoke to me in German, and to his sisters in English.

We took him to Trier, parking as close as we could to the Romanesque cathedral so that his steps would be as few as possible. We drove right past the coliseum, because stopping to look around would have taken more energy than he had. When we left my aunt's house after the second big family dinner, there were many emotional goodbyes to be said. He looked at me without recognition, shook my hand, and politely said his farewell.

"No Daddy, it's me," I said. "You're going home with me."

The last few days in his native country continued to sap his energy and awareness. We traveled to Cologne to see the cathedral because my father had told me in the weeks before we left that he had never been there and would like to visit. But once inside, he shuffled along at a snail's pace, looking neither left nor right. A one-year-old would have been more responsive, I thought sadly, with young and inquisitive eyes drawn instinctively to gleaming brass and brilliant stained glass.

I stopped him from time to time and placed my hands on his shoulders, turning him gently to face the splendid windows. "Look, Daddy, isn't that beautiful?" He would nod, and then the shuffle would resume. I turned the boys loose for a half hour to climb the cathedral spire, and my father and I sat in silence in one of the pews. Tourists and other faithful meandered around us slowly, awestruck, always looking up, their eyes drawn to arches and statuary and filigree and biblical stories captured in radiant glassworks. From what I remember, he looked mostly straight ahead.

By the time we left Frankfurt, headed again across the Atlantic, my father was ragged. He had been fêted and celebrated, guided and pampered every step of the way. But the uncertainty of his surroundings and the strain of travel had taken its toll. As we searched for our seats on the plane, he could not grasp why we could not take the first empty seats we saw. Where did all these people come from, he asked. Once seated, he thought he was in church. We commandeered a wheelchair for him upon landing, and his grandsons watched him like a hawk while I retrieved the car from the long-term parking a bus and a train ride away.

A year later, my father has returned to what passes for "normal" these days. He lets the dog out, makes a cup of tea, helps prepare dinner, listens to the radio. Sometimes he remembers things like the price of chocolate ten years ago, sometimes he forgets to lock the front door behind him. Despite the photo album and videocassette I made of our trip, I don't know how much of it he really remembers.

But I like to think...and I need to believe...that the fact that he stepped out of a shiny black Mercedes on Easter Sunday to the cobblestoned streets of his birthplace with two strapping grandsons and a smiling daughter in a polka-dot silk dress somehow... mattered.

And still lingers.

Thelma and Louise on Spring Break

One state west of us, the weather system we were driving through had turned deadly. More than a dozen people had died as a result of the storms we passed through that first day in Missouri, Kentucky and southern Illinois. My friend Kristin and I blithely made our way south, our minds on vacation, completely unaware. We had our favorite CDs playing on the stereo system and a can of Diet Coke apiece.

At the time, all we knew was that the windshield wipers on the rental car went "bumpety, bumpety, bumpety" every time they dragged across the glass for nine hours straight; the car's steering had a definite "float" to it, especially in the wind; and the water in the drainage channels beside the two-lane road we were on was getting a wee bit high.

The sign at the Dairy Queen where we stopped to freshen up looked like it would be under water soon. Raindrops broke the surface of the gleaming black pool surrounding it, and lights from a nearby gas station shimmered off the rising water. At the rate we were going, all we knew was that we were never going to make it to our motel reservation in Montgomery, Alabama before three a.m. And so we settled for a cheap room in Birmingham, scoring a double room on our third try after midnight.

Welcome to spring break. Or "Girls Gone Mild."

The first day of midlife adventure had started off with not much to recommend it. Thick, cottony fog cloaked most of the first leg of my trip from Wisconsin to Peoria, Illinois, where Kristin and I had agreed to meet for the rest of this spur-of-the-moment adventure. The fog had slowed me down by about an hour, and the fact that I hadn't looked up any directions to the Peoria airport before leaving added another. Really, I'd thought smugly, how hard could it be to find an airport in Peoria? For that matter, how big could Peoria really be? A lot bigger than I had thought. And the kindness of strangers is no substitute for a detailed map.

No matter, Kristin and I were on "spring break" and nothing was going to break our good mood. Sense and sensibility had no parts to play. We were fed up with winter, pure and simple, and we were goin' south.

Winter had been long and ghastly in our neck of the woods, which roughly sketched would cut a swath across Iowa, Minnesota, Illinois and Wisconsin. There had been snowstorm after snowstorm. School cancellation after school cancellation. Temperatures below zero. Days that I dutifully drove the fifty miles to work only to desperately wish—halfway there and fishtailing on snow-covered roads—that I had stayed safely home in bed, cocooned in flannel sheets.

And the winds and the grey skies just kept coming. It felt, deep down and for the first time that I could remember, as if I would never see spring or green grass again. As if I was living on a polar ice cap, and that flowers were something to be admired only in catalogs, grown by happy shirt-sleeved gardeners in tropical warm, sunny places thousands of miles south.

By early March, something in me had snapped and I became a desperate woman. Apparently the malaise was catchy. Kristin and I charged off the blocks only four days after I broached the idea. She—living a good six hours away in Iowa—sold her husband on the idea that she really needed a winter break too, and that he and their two daughters could spare her attentions for a few days.

Our plan was simple. We would meet and drive straight south until we hit the Gulf of Mexico, stopping at the first beach we found. And it actually worked. About the time we were sixty miles from Gulf Shores, Alabama, the clouds finally parted, the sun came out, and we saw blue skies above. And sure enough, when we finally ran out of road, it ended in a public parking lot at the edge of a pure, white sand beach. Enormous breakers kicked up spray a few hundred feet from where we stood. We locked the car, rolled up our pants, and happily waded in. We'd made it. It was about damned time.

If you'd look back at my college years, you'd know that I had never properly been on "spring break" before. While my friends and classmates piled on to chartered buses and into cars and sped south in the middle of March, I was working. And after I married and started a family, herding four kids, a husband, six suitcases and a hidden stash of Easter chocolate to a vacation condo on the shore just did not qualify.

The words "spring break" just enjoyed a connotation of more carefree abandon, of caution thrown to the wind, of randomness and adventure and opportunity and the Great Unknown. Of course, they also conjured up popular visions of "Girls Gone Wild" and drunken revelry and bikini-ready hardbodies oiled up and ready for Mai Tais and short-lived romances. But hey, I had to start somewhere.

There are advantages to doing some things when you're older. Sometimes it's simply that you know, starting out, that your friendship is strong enough to survive a two-day cramped, muscle-screaming drive of twelve hundred miles in a compact car. In our case, the catching up we did during the drive was half the adventure. Kristin and I had weathered law school together, with all its paranoia and all-or-nothing semester exams and anxiety and pressure and competition and chocolate cravings. Since graduating, Kristin and her family had moved twice. I had gotten divorced and adjusted to all that that big change brings. And between the two of us, fully half our children had weathered serious health crises and major surgeries. Not to take anything away from the incredible courage and grace and resilience of our children in dealing with these horribly inequitable turns of chance...but that kind of bad luck gives two mothers a lot to talk about as the miles roll by.

Another advantage to being oh, let's say...over thirty...is that you don't feel you've got to reinvent the wheel and discover everything for yourself to make great memories. I had picked Gulf Shores as a destination because a clerk at the courthouse suggested that it would be a nice place to visit, and a two-minute search on the internet later that night had me sold. Walking on the beach that first evening, we struck up a conversation with a local and asked him where we might find a good seafood restaurant. He directed us right up the street to a place with a full parking lot and a dolphin statue outside. And boy, was he right on the money!

The next morning, with a full day to make the most of, Kristin slept in. I wound up sharing breakfast with an elderly gentleman from Illinois who buttonholed me in the parking lot. His wife was a late sleeper too. One pearl of wisdom he imparted was how to find the tourist welcome center in town. I had blindly driven past it twice in the dark the night before. A clerk at the welcome center, asked for the best, quietest beach around, pointed us to her personal favorite, Cotton Bayou Beach a few miles down the coast. Just to say we did, we drove past it by a few miles and into Florida looking for something better...and then turned right around. We also took her advice about where to eat near the beach too. As the day drew to a close, we wolfed down plate after plate of seafood appetizers, foregoing entirely the niceties of a full dinner (rolls, salad, potatoes, veggies) in favor of crabmeat and shrimp and grilled tuna from start to finish. And after dinner, as we walked along the shore and watched the full moon shimmer on the water, we never regretted not wasting our time looking for "something better."

The beach alone had been worth the trip. The shore was famous for its pure white "sugar sand." The rise and fall of waves rushing in was a primal rhythm. And the chorus of black-faced laughing gulls behind us sounded like a bunch of raucous monkeys in a tree. As I walked along the water's edge, stopping to pick up the occasional small, perfect shell, I felt very much like the little girl I used to be, bent over and searching with single purpose for tiny shells along the edge of Lake Michigan in Chicago as the sun beat down on my back.

Anne Morrow Lindbergh got it exactly right in her inspiring book of essays, "Gift from the Sea," when she wrote that "the beach is not the place to work; to read, write or think." I have forgotten that many times over the years, and brought notebooks and pens and lists and good intentions to the shore as she once had, expecting to find the inspiration to write, only to find myself mesmerized by the sound of the waves and the wind. It feels like listening to the world breathe. Even this time, I had efficiently packed both a book and a magazine in my tote bag—Dan Brown's "Angels and Demons" and the latest Oprah magazine. Really, you couldn't ask for lighter, less demanding beach reading than that! And yet I still found myself hypnotized by my surroundings. The book and the magazine remained untouched as I stretched out full-length and dug my fingers into the warm, perfect sand around me.

Instead of "accomplishing" anything, Kristin and I shopped just a little for souvenirs to bring home. Mostly, we stretched out on the shore, waking only long enough to turn over and broil our other sides. Basking like lizards in the sun, we felt the energy of the universe permeate our frozen bone marrow and imprint our shivering psyches with memories of warmth that would have to last us the rest of the winter. With two blankets and plenty of sunblock, there was nothing essential that we lacked. We snacked our way through the days, nibbling on seafood dip and crackers we brought in a picnic cooler with hummus, and goat cheese, and grapes, and fancy chocolates, and unspecified beverages which may or may not have contained alcohol in violation of local ordinance.

And about that ordinance... While the signs posted at the edge of the beach all warned that alcoholic beverages were utterly forbidden, well. We were females over the age of thirty in bathing suits relaxing on a public beach, while college kids with much better bodies in far skimpier bathing suits frolicked and played Frisbee and volleyball nearby.

In other words, we were absolutely invisible. *A votre santé!* Having left our only bottle opener—my Swiss Army knife—in the hotel room, Kristin knowingly drew on what she called her "sketchy past" and taught me how to open a long-necked bottle with a house key. It is *never* too late to learn a new social skill.

Two days at the shore passed far too quickly by any measure. We skipped a trip to a nearby outlet mall—completely out of character for us—in favor of spending the last few hours on the beach. When the time came, we packed up and left straight from the shore, with sand in our shoes and the windows down, the sound of the waves and the laughing gulls fading behind us. The drive back was dry this time, but at two full days, still far too long for comfort.

We split again at the Peoria airport, with a shuffle of bags and a quick hug before beginning our last sprints back toward reality. In my case, reentering the "real world" meant serving Easter dinner for eight at my house the next day…and a mad dash to the supermarket on Easter morning for something to cook. Fifteen inches of fresh snow that had fallen at my house the day we left Alabama welcomed me back.

But I brought a piece of the shore back with me. Literally. Before we left, I scooped a few handfuls of that lovely sugar sand into a plastic grocery bag, and added a half dozen tiny shells in colors of grey and white and tangerine. Now encased in a glass jar and wrapped with a shimmery ribbon the color of sea foam, a miniature version of the Gulf of Mexico sits on my desk at work. The swirls of the seashells draw me hypnotically back to the rhythm of the shore, and remind me daily of the value of acting on impulse once in a while

And if I ever need a deeper dose of those memories but can't quite manage a getaway to a warm shore…I can always read "Gift from the Sea" once more.

May it Please the Court

"May it please the court."

The words are enough to strike terror into the hearts of most attorneys I know. They are the first words you speak when you address the Wisconsin Supreme Court in an oral argument. The words are ritual, standardized and formal. And I was about to say them myself…if I just didn't faint.

I have a framed photo on my desk at work. It dates from perhaps a year before I started law school at the age of forty, and only a few months before I would break my back in a riding accident, spend three painful months in a body cast, and have the world as I knew it divide into "before" and "after."

In the photo, I am standing in a winter woods, with my four children gathered around me. They range, in that picture, from about three years old to thirteen. We are surrounded by pristine snow and bare trees, and framed in a pretty fieldstone archway. I am beaming, and my entire universe revolves around keeping them safe and warm and out of harm's way.

If you had walked up to me then and told me that in just a few short years I would not only be a criminal prosecutor but find myself arguing cases before the state supreme court, I would have given you the same stare as if you'd told me that I was really the Queen of England, and a Lear jet was standing by to whisk me back across the pond. Oh, and the roof at Buckingham Palace needs fixing.

I might have smiled pleasantly, rolled my eyes...and then called the police.

But fate—and a tall horse who steered like a barge— intervened, and barely a year after I was lifted off the sandy soil of a riding arena on a back board, my youngest son started part-time kindergarten and I started law school as one of the first part-time students enrolled at Marquette University Law School. I remember sitting in a large classroom during orientation week, surrounded by dozens of twenty-somethings literally young enough to be my children. An affable professor at the front of the room was demonstrating the Socratic method of teaching with an exercise that kicked off with the question, "who owns the moon?"

I didn't really care about the moon right then, but as he spoke I felt an oppressive cloud of pessimism descend on me like a starless night.

What was I thinking? How could I possibly survive this? How could I compete with kids who had no families to care for and no pets and no responsibilities, who could close the law library and then go out for drinks and convivially debate legal theory over pitchers of beer, who could read textbooks with their breakfast cereal? In contrast, I had four kids, a dog, two elderly horses, and a marriage that was teetering on the verge of collapse. My sense of doom right then was as deep and all-consuming as a black hole.

But on the ride home, I reminded myself that I'd already borrowed the money for the first year...and I might as well toughen up and show up for class the following week.

I soon found a comforting road rhythm in driving the thirty miles to school three times a week. I studied like crazy for four hours every Friday morning, kept ferrying children as usual to tennis and soccer and gymnastics and volleyball, and skipped class whenever there was a field trip or it was my turn to be the "hot dog mom" at the grade school. And somehow, through it all, I managed to achieve a very good grade point average.

There was one serious barrier for me to conquer, though. All my life I had suffered from a tremendous, crippling fear of public speaking. Call it panic attacks, anxiety attacks, sheer nerves, I was unable to get up in front of a room full of people without my heart racing and my breathing going tight and shallow, and my voice shaking with dread. I will never forget the first time I was called on to "brief" a case in front of a law class.

Standing near the back row of an amphitheater classroom, I could feel the cold wind of fear and desperation creeping up my back, and while I knew the subject well, I barely choked out the words with great difficulty. The professor sat, motionless, on the edge of his desk at the front of the room. I have often imagined what must have been going through his mind. Two things, probably. First, if I died of fright, what on earth would he tell the dean? And second, what on earth would he do with the body?

After that first debacle, I forced myself to confront my demons. In every single class after that, I read ahead and raised my hand, determined to say something on point. Little by little, with every attempt, my heart quit pounding quite so hard, and my voice stopped quavering so much.

Still, it was a decidedly uphill climb. When the rest of my classmates showed up conservatively dressed in suits for our first mini "oral arguments" day in a legal writing class, I showed up in jeans and a Mother's Day T-shirt that read "Best Mom in the Whole World." I wore it to remind me that if I fell flat on my face in school, I still had a life. If I had to do that day over, I'd still wear the same thing.

Three-and-a-half years after I started, I finally graduated from law school with honors and a commitment to finding a job as a criminal prosecutor. I was lucky enough to quickly land a part-time position with the District Attorney's office in Sheboygan, Wisconsin. The post was newly created, and both my boss and I were open to suggestions as to how to make the best use of my time.

As a former journalist, I naturally gravitated to writing projects—briefs, motions, research, appeals. And then one fine day one of the other attorneys in the office turned up at my desk with several pounds of paper for me to review. He had won a TPR

("Termination of Parental Rights") case at trial before a jury, but the judge had subsequently refused to terminate the mother's rights based on a technicality. What did I think?

I had been a prosecuting attorney for less than a year. I had never looked at the Children's Code before this. But I rolled up my sleeves, read the statutes and the judge's decision, and came to the conclusion that the judge had gotten it wrong. My boss gave me the green light to file an appeal.

A few months later, the written decision came down from the Court of Appeals. The appellate judge ruled in favor of the trial court judge. Once again, several pounds of paper landed with a thump on my desk. What did I think? We had now lost the case twice in a row…but when I looked at the law and the appellate court's reasoning, I came to the conclusion that *this* decision was wrong too. I got another green light, this time to go knocking on the door of the state supreme court. My "petition for review" was granted. And I was absolutely terrified.

All of my old fears of speaking before an audience came flooding back, in spades. As a survival mechanism, my obsessive compulsive streak kicked in then, and I zealously over-prepared. Terrified that I might not have an answer, or that my mind might just go blank, I researched…and rehearsed…and researched some more.

The stakes were high, as they always are at this level of argument. On a personal level, the case came down to whether a three-year-old boy who had been placed in foster care for very

60

good reasons could be freed up for adoption by the family who wanted him. On a broader plane, the issue that would be decided for this case and all cases coming after it was just when in the formal TPR process the courts should stop favoring a parent's right to stay connected and start considering the "best interest of the child."

Since the case involved a young child who clearly deserved a better life, the "mother tiger" in me kicked in as well and I spent extra time on weekends working on the case. As ideas came to me while I was driving, I pulled over to the side of the road to jot them down on Dairy Queen napkins. I sat cross-legged on the cold floor of the courthouse basement, poring over dusty statute books from the 1800s, trying to trace the path in the law from when children were considered property to the realities and priorities of the present day.

I rehearsed my introduction over and over again as I drove, afraid that if I didn't have the words—including my name—absolutely committed to some subconscious part of my brain stem, I might freeze like a deer in the headlights.

And finally the day came to argue before the high court. I had brought my older son with me for company. I treated him to lunch beforehand at an Italian restaurant. I passed on his offer to share his breadsticks, and took another dose of Pepto Bismol to steady my nervous stomach. My friend and co-worker who had tried the case in the local circuit court joined us. As he sat beside me at the counsel table in the packed room, I told him "if I pass out, just pick up my notes and keep reading!" I wasn't kidding.

As the person who had asked the high court to hear the case, it was my turn to go first. The justices filed into the courtroom in their black robes, and solemnly took their seats. One of the justices and I had been reporters at the same newspaper many years earlier, and she gave me a quick smile as our eyes met. I don't recall that it made me feel any less nervous.

As I began to speak, I could feel my chest start to tighten and my air supply go dangerously short. My voice shook for a bit, but it passed. I remembered that what was at stake was far more important than what I was afraid of, and my breathing finally returned to normal as the justices started to pepper me with questions about the case and the law.

Gratitude and relief beyond words flooded through me when I finally got to sit down and turn the hot seat over to the attorney on the other side. When the arguments were finally over, my son and my friend and I left the courthouse and stepped out into the sunlight. As I cleared the doorway, I looked at the sky and declared, "Thank God I'll never have to do that again!!" I was absolutely sure that I wouldn't survive another round.

The three of us headed to a nearby restaurant for a little celebration. We settled in to our air-conditioned seats, and ordered drinks and nachos. As we waited, I repeated my heartfelt desire to avoid such an incredibly grueling experience again.

My friend looked at me and smiled wickedly. "You know, I've got another case I want you to look at..." Oh dear God.

Timelines for appeals in cases involving TPRs are mercilessly short. I wouldn't have thought it possible at first, but only five weeks later—and months before the first case was even decided—I had finished another brief and had it sitting in the supreme court's "in" box. And I went on to prepare and argue three *more* cases to the court after that.

Then I finally got to catch my breath. Even now, the thought of saying the words "May it please the court" can make my heart race.

As for that first case...the decision eventually came down months later in our favor, with the vote being a clean sweep of seven to nothing. I like to say that the good guys won, and just leave it at that.

But win or lose, every time I look at that picture from the snowy woods...I think about how far I've traveled.

Cookie Therapy

From a distance, I didn't have much to complain about. I was stretched out on one end of a comfy recliner sofa. There was a cat curled up behind me on the bay window sill, and a new car in the garage. I had just enjoyed a good dinner. I had a good job, good friends, a solid roof over my head, you know the drill. And then, despite the doors and windows and screens tightly closed...the past crept in, without knocking.

My youngest son sat on the far edge of the recliner, the golden glow of the floor lamp falling on him as he read. The television was on, and he was surrounded by books and folders, pens and papers. He nestled in to his comfortable corner, intently digging in to the first semester of his junior year. The biggest change for him at that moment was that now he was driving himself to school.

They say—whoever "they" are—that your past comes back to haunt you when your children turn the same age that you were when life sideswiped you and left you careening down a different path than the one you expected.

This was my "caboose" baby—the last of the lot—sitting here studying, blissfully unaware at the age of sixteen of his mother's sudden, stumbling trip down memory lane. When his siblings were older and hit that milestone, I was too busy to notice. One, then another, then another turned sixteen, and I kept the plates spinning in the air with little time for reflection. Soccer games, tennis meets, football helmets, potluck dinners, practices, homework, ear infections, summer camps, tests, prom dress shopping, family vacations at the shore. Introspection...who had the time?

I did now.

Whatever had passed for "normal" as I was growing up on the northwest side of Chicago—traffic noise, Catholic school uniforms in various plaids, city bus schedules, homework, science fairs, French club, knowing that the bed you went to sleep in would still be there a month later—went out the window when I was sixteen. I came home from a six-week study trip to Europe with my high school history teacher and a busload of classmates in the summer between sophomore and junior year to find that my parents had gone "off the reservation" and moved to an abandoned farm in northern Wisconsin. They had bought the property a few years earlier "as an investment." I don't remember moving. I don't remember packing. I don't remember leaving the city. I don't remember arriving at the farm. But somehow, I was just there.

The nearest town was two miles away, with a population of 143. I remember a feed mill, a tiny post office, a softball field, a church. It probably had a bar or two or three, but we didn't mingle much. Our isolation from the larger world was near total. We had no television reception, no daily newspapers, no newsmagazines, and only two channels that reached us on the radio—country/western and National Public Radio. The red brick house was missing a front porch and had no indoor plumbing except for a kitchen sink. The place had not been lived in for years, and it appeared that the window on the north side of the kitchen had once served as a garbage chute into the yard. On one of their earlier reconnaissance trips, my parents had purchased two calves and a pony before we built fences or even moved in. We spent a lot of time chasing this trio from the open fields back to the barn.

They ordered a couple of dozen chicks from the feed mill, and we raised a flock of Leghorn hens and a pair of roosters. In summer, two of the hens—never say these birds weren't smart—casually loitered like delinquents near the kitchen door, then dashed inside when it opened to steal food from the dog's dish. Occasionally they made it as far as the butter dish on the kitchen table before they were scooped up and unceremoniously tossed back outside, fluffing their feathers in indignation.

When the weather turned colder, the chickens moved from the coop into the barn with the cow and the horses. When it got *really* cold and the points of their red combs started to turn black with frostbite, the chickens moved into the basement.

My father had grown up in a small farming village in Germany, and he clearly loved the place. With a hundred untilled acres at our disposal, he taught me to cut hay with a scythe and turn it over

66

with a pitchfork to dry. I unfortunately put a flat tire on the three-quarter-ton pickup truck one day when I inexpertly tried to back it up the barn ramp to the upper floor. The truck bed was filled with loose, fragrant hay, and the plan was working just fine until I steered a little too close to the edge of the ramp. The wheel rim cut into the soft rubber of the tire, and the tire went flat. After that, we finally started buying most of our hay in bales.

When winter's cold fury caused the water pipes in the barn to freeze, watering the animals became a grueling task. We started by filling five-gallon pails of water in the basement of the house. Then we toted them up the stairs to ground level before then navigating the slippery, snow-covered slope downward from the house, trying not to slosh or slip.

The menagerie grew in fits and starts—we bought or raised geese, ducks, a pig, a horse, and a Guernsey cow named Queenie. Queenie had a mild disposition, but she still came equipped with a set of long, curvy horns that scared me to death. We bought a calf at an auction and brought her home in the back seat of our bright yellow Matador. We called her Daisy. I learned to milk Queenie by hand the day she arrived, bucket between my knees, teetering on a tiny stool. We strained the milk through cheesecloth right into glass juice bottles, and then put it in the refrigerator. I still remember how a rich layer of cream rose to the top of the milk.

I managed to finish another year of high school through all the chaos, and then graduated at the end of my junior year. I stayed on the farm for another year, working occasionally as a waitress or a file clerk, shoveling mountains of manure, and baking a lot. I made pound cakes, layer cakes, white bread, wheat bread, chocolate chip cookies, and loaves of cinnamon bread with creamy white frosting. I kneaded the yeast dough to satiny, elastic balls on the wooden kitchen table. The ebb and flow of the rhythm was soothing in the midst of all the other hardships. I even tried my hand at making raised donuts, frying them in hot goose grease (yes, *those* geese!) and then rolling them in sugar. They actually didn't taste bad.

Time passed. I eventually left the farm and made my way to college. I got a degree, got married, started a family, and kept on baking. I'm from that generation that remembers those Poppin' Fresh Pillsbury Dough Boy commercials as gospel. I can still sing the jingle, *"Nothin' says lovin' like something from the oven, and Pillsbury says it best!"* And I still firmly believe that a little home baking can make just about anything better.

As the kids grew, I put this principle into practice often. Left with an hour before the school bus arrived in the afternoon to drop them off, I would survey the clutter in the house and weigh my options. I could straighten up the living room before they walked in, sure that any superficial neatness I imposed would begin to naturally unravel as soon as they arrived. Or I could reach for the chocolate chips. It was a no brainer. Nothing could compare to the sound of the front door opening, a footfall or two and the "thunk" of a school bag hitting the floor, then a tiny pause followed by the rapturous exclamation, *"ooooooooooh, you made COOKIES!!"*

Back in the present, after a few days of brooding and feeling strangely bereft of my moorings, I knew it was definitely cookie time. I got out the hand mixer, the chocolate chips, the butter, the vanilla, the eggs. Someone gave me an expensive, heavy KitchenAid stand mixer once, a wondrous, gigantic appliance that could perfectly blend all the ingredients for me while I did other things elsewhere in the kitchen. I used it twice to be polite, then moved it permanently to the basement.

There is a primitive, tactile joy to be found in pushing the ingredients around in the bowl, watching the raw materials blend and swirl and transform in stages into the finished product. The texture and color of this foundation change as each egg or square of melted chocolate or cup of sugar is factored in and combined into the whole. It is not unlike building a sand castle, or driving a bulldozer on a construction site, measuring your progress by the way the mound of dirt you're pushing around changes shape. If you could operate it by remote control, well, where's the fun in that?

I mixed. I scraped. I cheated (and risked salmonella poisoning) and defiantly ate the raw dough straight from the bowl the way I always did when I was younger. I dropped spoonfuls of chocolate-chip-laden dough on cookie sheets and then watched them zealously as they baked, whisking them out of the oven precisely when their edges turned light brown and their crowns began to look slightly crisp. My son cruised through the kitchen, and started to graze while the cookies were still warm. I divided up the rest into plastic storage containers—some for us, the rest for the older two kids we were was planning to see the next day.

I picked up the college kids, took them out to lunch, visited, caught up on subjects like school and life, and strong-armed one into buying some new shoes.

And then I brought out the home-baked offerings, love neatly sealed in a square Ziploc container. And again, there was that satisfying, familiar moment of recognition, that happy sound of *"oooooooooh,* you made ***COOKIES!!"***

I feel so much better already.

Tale of the Christmas Axes

Martha Stewart, stop reading right now. I can't be held responsible for the stroke sure to follow if you find out about Christmas at my house or at my friend Barb's house. It's all about what happens when you finally turn over the reins of control. In the end, you laugh a lot harder...but it doesn't sell many magazines.

Barb and I could be templates for that tired stereotype, "women who do too much." That's not because we're perfect, but because we're both coming from behind. Barb still has some recuperation issues from back and neck surgery that slow her down from time to time. And after a riding accident years ago, I still run out of steam—and the ability to just keep standing—on a long day faster than I used to. This doesn't keep either of us from pulling out all the stops at the holidays. I know Barb's usual standard for holiday decorating—warm and inviting and really pretty. Her tree is about twelve feet tall. Mine, well...not so much. But I do have my moments.

This time, I had three of my four children coming home from college or beyond right before Christmas, and I wanted the short

71

time they could all spend together to be as cozy as a Norman Rockwell picture turned into a Hallmark television movie.

There was a wreath on the door, and a nine-foot Christmas tree with dozens of glass-blown and hand-embroidered ornaments, strung with strings of red wooden "cranberries." It was festooned with a virtual aviary of ceramic birds and other woodland critters. There was homemade pumpkin pie, homemade banana muffins, and homemade Christmas cookies in four varieties. Needlepoint stockings hung by the chimney with care. I couldn't locate the crèche for the second year running, but I found the stuffed moose that sings "Grandma Got Run Over By a Reindeer" and put fresh batteries in him before they got home. Somebody sat on it as if on cue and the moose started to sing. There was sixty pounds of fresh firewood in the wrought iron stand next to the fireplace, along with a basket of "fatwood" to start the fire in a hurry. There was fresh coffee in the pot, and whipped cream to go on the hot chocolate.

Oh…did I mention that this was the first Christmas after the divorce?

The high point for traditional Christmas fun has always been rolling out and decorating the butter cookies. And this year was no exception. The kids set to the task almost as soon as Michael, a college freshman, walked in the door and dumped his gear. By the time he arrived it was late afternoon, and I was absolutely done in after days of shopping and wrapping and baking. And I had also fit in two days of working on a last-minute felony drug trial.

I poured myself a glass of wine, pulled the bowl of cookie cutters and the mixer down from the top shelf of the cabinet, and handed off the rolling pin to the younger generation. "Knock yourselves out," I said, and sat down on the sofa in the living room to read the paper as flames danced in the hearth.

The kitchen was a beehive of happy noise and activity, and I enjoyed the energy from a distance. As soon as the last batch of cookies was finished and cooling, we had dinner and ripped into our presents. Then the kids left to open gifts at their dad's house across town, and I finally began to take inventory of what they'd left behind.

It looked like a holiday bomb had gone off. Every open surface in the kitchen was covered with flour, or gingerbread crumbs, or frosting. There were red sugar crystals. Green sugar crystals. Candy hearts, candy sprinkles, and candy flowers. Discarded coffee cups and wine glasses were everywhere. Cookies were everywhere, too, and as I started to gently slide them off the cookie sheets to store them, I laughed out loud.

My late mother-in-law had given me the cookie cutters two decades before, and every year I had pulled out the most obvious holiday ones from the eclectic collection. There was a Santa, and an angel, a reindeer, a fir tree, a bell, a star, a heart, a flower. And every year, the maternal censor in me had stopped at pulling out the cookie cutter that was clearly shaped like an axe. Why Santa might need an axe on his journeys anyway, I could only guess. But the kids had found the axe-shaped cookie cutter in the bottom of the bowl I'd handed them, and had taken it to town.

There were lots and lots of Christmas axes in this year's cookie assortment. They were *bloody* axes, in fact, since they had decorated the edges of the blades with red sugar crystals. Keeping the theme going, they had brought the angels into the act as well, with bloody little angel hands to go with the bloody little axes. I was surprised they let Santa keep his head on his shoulders. The extra dreadlocks they added to Rudolph's antlers and colored red, making him the "Sideshow Bob" of the reindeer team, seemed almost like an afterthought. I packed cookies and laughed. Then I packed some more cookies, and laughed for the rest of the night.

The next day I called Barb to tell her about the new Christmas tradition. She had one of her own to match. She had apparently run out of holiday steam a bit early as well, and had turned the task of decorating the gingerbread men over to a twelve-year-old niece. Surprise! Her niece made an artistic judgment that gingerbread men looked better with three eyes than two. And a new tradition was born.

From now on, gingerbread men at Barb's house will have a third eye. And at my house, when the kids want to make bloody Christmas axes and murderous angels again, I'll make sure they've got red frosting to do the job right.

The Island

The feeling never gets old. As the ferry boat's engines roar to life and the boat pulls away from the dock, the weight of reality slips from your shoulders like a silk scarf caught by the breeze and carried away, vanishing like a magician's sleight of hand. Looking forward, from the vehicle deck closer to the water, the cold spray of dark waves cut by the ferry's prow is bracing, awakening. Looking backward, the endless woods surrounding the dock and leaning over the shoreline gradually diminish to nothing as the ferry gamely shoulders it way across Death's Door to Washington Island.

The journey was one of many I had taken over the years, but the first one I was making alone.

The first time I went to the island had been nearly twenty years before. My friend Liz had a family vacation cabin on the island, and invited me to bring my two young daughters to visit for a few days one summer. Her husband was in medical school, and she often took her own girls up there for extended stays, to the island where she had spent her summers as a child.

The trip was an odyssey. The sensible minivan was packed with two car seats, girls aged two and four, a chocolate chip cheesecake with a chocolate crumb crust, a four-pack of wine coolers, and other toys, accessories and accoutrements and beach toys for several days of fun.

We drove an unfamiliar route for hours, through the entirety of the enormous peninsula jutting like a thumb into Lake Michigan, all the way to land's end and the ferry dock where we waited for the next stage of the journey.

Fares paid, we followed like sheep as the single-file line of cars and trucks was guided one by one by the crew into four parallel lines on the boat, nearly bumper to bumper. Then, ignition turned off, we climbed the narrow metal stairs and settled in on a bench on the passenger deck. I clutched the girls in a death grip as the boat pulled away from the dock, afraid that they might lean too far over the side rail.

A half-hour later, with windblown hair, sunburned cheeks and a sense of absolute wonder, we disembarked and started following more of Liz's directions to the cabin. We drove several miles further north, then turned east and drove clear to the far eastern side of the island. Another turn north brought us to the outermost edge, down a gravel path through pines and hardwoods. The cabin sat in a clearing, with its white siding and red roof gleaming prettily in the sun.

Beyond the house was a bluff, and at the edge of the bluff, fifty-foot birch trees swayed, their leaves glinting in the afternoon sunlight. The waves on Lake Michigan waves glittered in the distance like diamond dust. The air was clear and pure. I felt like I had arrived at the gates of heaven.

For years after that maiden voyage, we returned to the island as a family for a week every summer, with two children, then three, then four. The days were lazy, spent mostly at the beach, with occasional forays to the island gift shops for souvenirs and ice cream. Eventually, though, the children outgrew the sense of wonder at finding yet another clam shell in the water, and we found other places to vacation. Once the inevitable dissonance of college scheduling clashed with the local school year for the younger ones, it became hard to schedule family vacations at all.

But here I was, heading back to the island again, wondering whether this was a good idea.

The island wasn't my first choice for this trip. The summer before, I had spent a week at a writer's retreat on the peninsula. It was nurturing, encouraging, inspiring, invigorating, thought-provoking...and it came with all meals included and wonderfully prepared. I had hoped to return to replenish my writer's soul, but found I could not get the necessary week off from work.

So I dried my tears, and resolutely booked a tiny affordable cabin on the island, on the water, for a week when I could get away from the office and when my sons, still living at home, would be out West in a camping adventure with their Dad. After the divorce, there would be no more family vacations of the old sort anyway.

I brought a laptop, my notebooks, a week's worth of frozen dinners, and a carton of Instant Breakfast packets. Heading north on the interstate, condensation collecting on the mocha frappuccino in the cup holder next to me, I had fleeting pangs of uncertainty about whether I could handle the solitude, the memories, the passage of time, the reminders of broken dreams.

I needn't have worried.

The cabin was tiny and prosaic. It had a small yard and a deck almost entirely surrounded by cedars, but with a clear line of sight from the back door across the deck, through the yard and to the shore beyond. If I parked myself just right on a lounge chair, with a Diet Coke next to me and my binoculars nearby, I could sit for hours and not leave the spot.

I wrote. I journaled. I read for the fun of it. I napped when I felt like it. I walked three miles every morning on quiet country roads that felt like cathedral naves. I bird watched with a passion. I drove into the tiny town in the middle of the island every day to pick up a copy of the Chicago Tribune, an ice cream bar and a candy bar, and then retreated to my fortress of solitude to read the newspaper on the deck.

I started the vacation by reading a few chapters of Henry David Thoreau's "Walden" on the first evening, putting me in an excellent frame of mind for appreciating nature. I re-read "Gift from the Sea" by Anne Morrow Lindbergh from cover to cover. From the deck I watched a bald eagle soar around a bird refuge on a tiny island nearby, and a broad-winged hawk depart my yard with a snake clutched in his talons. I watched a pair of mute swans and their two little cygnets swim around the refuge nearly every day.

In an interesting balancing of priorities, I weighed whether to show up for the open trap-shoot or attend a poetry reading/discussion group about Emily Dickenson, unfortunately scheduled for the same evening. Civility won out, although I felt a bit like a Neanderthal crashing an Edwardian dinner party. I had a terrific time nonetheless!

Despite the low lake level that summer, I finally found a shallow, crystalline, sand-bottomed bay in a nature preserve, and visited often, stretched out in the warm water while tiny quicksilver fish swam around me in curiosity. I watched an osprey return to land from hunting on the lake, his dinner suspended beneath him. I saw damselflies so brilliantly turquoise that I thought the first one was a piece of cast-off plastic, and dodged dragonflies the size of B-52s.

One evening, a bit tired of the flat, placid shoreline at my cabin, I went searching for crashing waves. I found them off Carlin's Point. It took a half-mile hike in from the road to the nature preserve, then another quarter-mile out across rocky, weedy flats where the shoreline used to be. Then I strode further across slimy rocks and weeds, and then across slippery, rocky shallows, until the water grew deeper and I finally felt waves crashing on my knees.

The wind nearly pushed me over, but it felt glorious. I stared in amazement as a seagull hovered above my right shoulder, brilliant white against the blue sky, suspended in this gale seemingly without effort.

Later, returning to the cabin, I watched a great blue heron fish out on a rocky islet, and felt an instant bond with a red-breasted merganser hen and her thirteen little ducklings who hung around my shoreline. Through all the years I had been ferrying my children back and forth, I had always said I felt like a mother duck.

The week passed quickly. I had spent basically every minute of good weather outdoors, face down on the lounge chair on the deck or face down on a blanket in a dune at the shore. There was only the sound of the waves in the distance and the wind up close, sunlight dappling through birch trees and cedars, birds singing nearby, and the feeling of being hooked up to some giant life support system that was pumping something vital back into me.

The end of a trip to the island always comes, not when you return home, but when the tires of your car finally grab pavement on the mainland as you drive off the ferry. This time was no different. But as I meandered my way home, on no particular time-table, so relaxed I was still nearly boneless, I thought...

Yes, the island was a good idea.

Riding Pillion

If I had had a list of what I was looking for in a man, owning a motorcycle wouldn't have just been down at the bottom, it wouldn't have made the list at all. Truth be told, it would even have tipped the balance the other way. I don't like loud engines. I have no sense of balance. I get dizzy on a step ladder if I'm a foot off the floor. I'm a control freak. And on and on.

But there I was, at the tail end of what I call "the year of turbo dating," metaphorically ready to take a step back and enter a convent for a while. And then there *he* was. Intelligent, intriguing, good looking and unconventional, the proud owner of both a longbow and a Harley. And so I threw caution to the wind and said "yes" to a first date.

The motorcycle was such a non-issue at the time. I live in Wisconsin, and when we met it was the middle of January. I can't remember if I wore long underwear on our first date, but I most certainly wore it on our second. Along with shearling-lined lug-soled boots, ear muffs, and a goose down parka trimmed with coyote fur. The wind chill was twenty-five below zero that night as

I drove to meet him for dinner and a movie, far removed from motorcycle weather up here. We routinely have potholes and boilerplate ice up here that can take out a car.

I also remember taking stock of the ridiculously, dangerously cold weather and thinking "girl, you're in trouble here!" But still…most of my dating for the past year had been "catch and release" after the first encounter, and the "curse of the third date" still lurked out there. There was no need to worry about riding on the motorcycle months hence when we might be calling it quits over dessert.

By the time the warm days of spring finally rolled around, I had been caught, hook, line and sinker. His enthusiasm for biking had always been palpable, but now it was edging into my future as well. I couldn't hang out on the tailgate of his pickup truck forever. I kept ducking the issue. But the day of reckoning finally arrived.

I had offered to take him out to dinner to celebrate a life-altering, monumental gardening project we had recently finished around my house. The garden was entirely his idea. The "before" was nothing short of a wasteland. The "after" saw me walking in beauty every time I stepped out the front door. In between, we had shoveled more than two tons of gravel by hand together, and replaced it with perennials and rose bushes and bark and sandstone. My life was forever changed.

And now, to get to the restaurant, he wanted to take the Harley.

Still, I dressed for a different occasion, hoping that some shred of caution—check the weather, thunderstorms possible later!—would keep the bike in the garage and our transportation involving four wheels and a roof. I wore blue plaid capri pants and a fluttery white see-through shirt over a skinny white tank top. I wore sandals and bare ankles.

The man and the Harley arrived on time, the bike gleaming in the sunlight, the man grinning and triumphant with anticipation. We sat on lawn chairs in the yard for a while, admiring the new and improved landscape, and I catalogued all the drawbacks I could think of.

I have trust issues. I will be the first to admit that I am a control freak. And I play by the rules, virtually all of the time. I never go in the "out" door, even when it's closer and it's standing wide open. Speed scares me to death, unless I'm the one driving. I'm terrified of heights, and I have absolutely no sense of balance. Stiletto heels are all the altitude I need. I like traveling in cars. I specifically like cars with air conditioning, and CD players, and cup holders for my Starbucks coffee, and air bags.

He listened patiently, then once again eloquently described his love of riding on his Harley. There was the freedom. The sensation of the wind on your skin, and all of nature around you. The magnificent sound. And he promised to keep to the speed limit. Then he reached into a storage compartment and thoughtfully brought out a spare helmet and his good black leather jacket. I tried it on.

With the plaid capri pants and sandals, I looked ridiculous. I exited stage left, and returned more suitably attired. Dark jeans, black high-heeled boots. I ditched the foofy white shirt in favor of something snug and knit. Then I shrugged into the jacket, put on the helmet, and taking pains to not nick the gas tank with the heel of my boot as I swung my leg over, positioned myself to ride pillion. In truth, the battle had been lost before it was even joined.

With a couple of basic instructions—lean into the turns with him or stay neutral instead of leaning the other way, loosen my death grip just a little so he could both breathe and drive—we took off slowly down the driveway and made it safely and without fanfare or hysteria to the restaurant three miles away. I remember I couldn't bring myself to even look over his left shoulder at oncoming traffic. But as some old friends entered the restaurant and met my guy before dinner arrived, I confess to a certain thrill at nodding at the motorcycle gleaming in the sunlight through the window next to me, and saying "yeah, that's my ride!"

Both we and the bike are now a few years older, and quite a few more miles have passed beneath the tires of the Harley with me on board. I went out and bought my own black leather jacket, after finally coming to grips with the fact that my chest is bigger than his. I've become accustomed to looking over at what's on the left side of the road now, as well as just looking up at the clouds and the trees and the birds above me as the wind slides over my face.

The smell of damp evergreens on a winding two-lane road feels as intoxicating to me as any glass of champagne. One summer evening I watched a flaming sunset sky unfold behind us in the rearview mirrors as we drove east into twilight. It was magic.

I used to think that sex was the final frontier in human intimacy, measured in hushed and sacred increments of trust, and closeness, and sharing, and vulnerability. I was wrong. You can make a whole lot of whoopee and still hold much of yourself back, hide those private places you don't want to share, feel like you're still somehow in control. The much bigger leap of raw faith and reliance is getting on the back of a motorcycle, wrapping your arms around someone's waist, and with a touch wordlessly conveying, "here's my life, I'm trusting you to keep me safe." I'm glad I figured that out.

Life has gotten in the way of riding much lately. Details like basement flooding and roof repairs and replacing the ring gear on the lawn tractor can take a bite out of leisure time. And as we are well aware, both life and relationships hold no guarantees.

But that black motorcycle jacket hangs in the closet nearest the front door, a reminder of miles spent already with my arms around his waist, circled by the familiar smell of pipe smoke and leather, and holding the promise of open road once again.

In terms of "take me away" moments...it sure beats a bubble bath.

"Alles Klar"

I thought briefly about packing the shotgun, but the car was nearly full and I was exhausted with a hundred and twenty miles yet to drive. Having any sort of a weapon in a house with an elderly ex-soldier with dementia issues never sounds like the brightest of ideas during daylight, no matter how "dodgy" the neighborhood. I also left the chain saw behind. Not that I'm sure I couldn't find a use for it.

The car was packed to the brim with my vacuum cleaner, my tool kit (with hex wrenches *and* two types of screwdrivers), the cordless drill, extra plates and silverware, and clothes for colder weather than what I'd worn the recent night I had blasted down to Chicago like a bat out of hell. I had extra movies on DVD, my latest Oprah magazine, a winter jacket, gloves and, of course, my Swiss Army knife. I also brought my plain black suit and heels, equally appropriate for either a funeral or a court appearance. Up next—stops at a nearby hardware store for a replacement part for an ancient broken doorknob; the local gas station where "regular unleaded" goes for fifty cents less a gallon than it does in Chicago;

a pit stop at Starbucks for some caffeine and a comfort zone; and a cruise through the racks of Best Buy looking for DVDs of Lawrence Welk and the Jackie Gleason show. I didn't find them, but at least I tried.

When I finally pulled out of town, the late afternoon sky was starting to darken, heralding temps below freezing just ahead. The setting sun blazed gold from behind swaths of grey and silver clouds to the west, while the three-quarter moon glared brightly like a chunk of ice in the clear eastern sky. Squadrons of geese flew overhead, and a hawk soared over the interstate, utterly unconcerned with the myriad human dramas unfolding below him at seventy miles an hour across six lanes of traffic.

I was headed back to Chicago, my home town, for the worst of all possible reasons.

The first frantic dash had come just a few days before. One minute I was sitting at my desk at work, pushing my way through a never-ending pile of paper. The next minute, my cell phone rang with the news that my elderly mother, already in a wheelchair most of the time, had fallen and badly fractured her thigh. My equally elderly father, incredibly feeble and showing symptoms of both Parkinson's and cognitive impairment, needed full-time care and supervision while the medical crisis unfolded.

And so I went, and waited, and talked with doctors and social workers and administrators and nurses, and tried to reassure my father that all would eventually be well. This last was a Herculean task. He and my mother had been married for fifty years and shared this apartment for the past thirty. His anxiety was palpable.

In the coming days, I tag-teamed him with my mother's two sisters—one with a bad leg and a psychotic Dalmatian; the other, the youngest, married to a former firefighter who, in his eighties, proved to be a Rock of Gibraltar every evening as we showed up at their house for dinner and a movie like orphans in a storm. With my father's limited mobility and attention span, we watched a lot of TV and movies.

We took in Gunsmoke episodes, laughed at the Three Stooges, and guffawed at the mud-splattered antics of George Clooney and his football team in the movie "Leatherheads." I tried hard to find movies in German, his native tongue, but turned up only two. One, "Schultze Gets the Blues," was so slow paced we switched it off…but not before my father surprised me by singing along in German with the characters in a scene..

We also watched Wolfgang Petersen's wrenching WWII epic "Das Boot" again. We had first shared it the summer before, when he had came to my house for a weekend visit. Seeing it again reinforced my beliefs that first, the movie is a genuine classic with a thrilling, haunting musical score, a "must see" for film buffs even with only English subtitles; and second, Jürgen Prochnow, the actor playing the stoic, nuanced submarine commander, is the most compelling actor I've ever seen on screen. And that includes Russell Crowe in "Gladiator," Viggo Mortenson in "Hidalgo," and Cary Grant in just about anything.

Just to get out of the house one day for a trip that didn't involve the hospital, I loaded my father into the car and took him to the Garfield Park Conservatory. There, under glass, was a riot of exotic chrysanthemums and bizarre succulents and lush foliage. We stopped for a while by the indoor pond that boasted a variety of ornamental carp and enormous glass waterlilies created by the artist Dale Chihuly. I had seen thousands of Chihuly's colorful glass flowers famously gracing the ceiling of the lobby of the Bellagio Hotel in Las Vegas in a more carefree time.

I restrained myself from physically yanking the trio of folks seated on the only bench near the water's edge, and reminded myself that under the circumstances, I was lucky to be here with my father at all.

We drove through Humboldt Park in our old neighborhood, where I used to bike and swing and sled as a child, and where he and I had searched for lost marbles as we walked in the woods. We cruised past the field house, and by the park's formal gardens and pool flanked by the pair of magnificent bronze bison originally designed for the 1893 World's Fair.

As we drove through the park, my father suddenly remembered the neighborhood bakery, Roeser's, and so we stopped there too. We bought a loaf of rye bread and a butter coffee cake smothered with icing.

As my mother made steady improvement with her recuperation in the hospital, my travels with my father took on less of an air of urgency and desperation. Often we listened to music as

I drove, but sometimes he would give me a short impromptu lesson in German. I would have to lean close to hear him, because his speech is no longer clear.

My mother continues to make progress, and the coming days are fraught with uncertainty as to the future for both of them.

But every night, as I have since this crisis began, I tuck my father into bed with the words "Guten nacht, mein Papa." Then I kiss him on the cheek and tell him "alles klar." Roughly translated, it means "everything's fine." He smiles and closes his eyes and I turn out the lights.

Alles klar. At least for this night.

Ripple Effect

She looked familiar but, somehow, shorter. For an embarrassing instant, I couldn't remember her name. But she was grabbing me by both elbows and smiling and anybody could tell she was *really* happy to see me!

I was standing in the middle of Miss Katie's Diner, a retro-fifties restaurant near Marquette University with a whole lot of steel and chrome, waitresses in bobby sox, and cheeseburgers that can make your mouth water. I had just finished lunch during a break from an annual criminal law conference that some of the guys from work and I go to every December to find out just how much we don't know about our jobs. Our little foursome stood up and shrugged into our coats, heading for the door. We looked like a casual, weekend version of the intro to "Law & Order." I turned, and then a gal I just knew that I knew from somewhere was right in front of me, brimming with good news.

"It's me, Cheryl," she said, and it suddenly all came back. She looked shorter because this time I was in boots with three-inch stacked heels instead of sneakers. "I just had to tell you, I'm graduating from Marquette this weekend with a double major, and it's all because of you!"

What??

We swapped essentials in a hurry, because I had to get back to the conference. My boss was driving, and while he's a terrific guy, he has never been known for his patience. But...she wasn't kidding. And I completely understood why. I had just been the messenger.

We had been soccer moms many years before, with children in preschool and grade school together. I hadn't seen her in years, but then we had bumped into each other by chance while I was running an errand between my law school classes. She was working at the university. We walked and talked one day on campus soon after, and caught up on what our children were doing. She confessed that she was tied up in knots about whether she should start taking classes toward a college degree. Tuition would be free because of her job at the university.

She could think of a million reasons that it would be too hard, too inconvenient for everybody else in the family, too complicated. And, of course, she felt she was "too old." I—bearing in mind that one of the ways I juggled law school with four kids at home was to remember that I could always buy clean socks and underwear at Walmart, open twenty-four hours a day—urged her to go for it. But the argument that clinched the deal, apparently, was something my long-departed grandmother had told my Aunt Patsy years ago when my aunt was agonizing over whether to study accounting.

Grandma was a poorly educated but quick witted and tart-tongued Irish immigrant with a very practical bent.

"You're going to be fifty years old whether you have that accounting degree or not," she said. "So why don't you turn fifty with it?" My aunt took that encouraging ass-kicking advice, got her CPA, and went to work for the Internal Revenue Service, gleefully making life hell for tax cheats. I will always remember the story. And so, apparently, will Cheryl.

We laughed and hugged each other at the diner, and then I left. My head was spinning for a long time, and it had nothing to do with trying to fold my five-foot-ten-in-heels frame into the back of the Jeep. It had everything to do with the power of a kind word and a little encouragement, and what had brought me this far.

I often think that we're all just living in the middle of a giant three-dimensional pinball machine, thrown from one trajectory to another by things entirely unpredictable. But one thing that remains constant is the remarkable power of believing in someone, and telling them about it. You just never know where that's going to make them end up.

For me, serendipity threw me off the full-time mommy track and on the path to law school at a tourist bar in Florida. I was on vacation with my two-year-old son and some relatives on Sanibel Island, and had arranged to have lunch with a guy I hadn't seen in seventeen years. We had reconnected because of a college reunion newsletter. John was working in Florida, and so one day he drove to the island and we caught up. Many years earlier, he had been a really bright, challenging, dissatisfied and angry young man, and had dropped out—or been kicked out—of school. I had always thought that his potential was limitless, and so before he left I bought him a poster to take along. It read "If you set your sights among the heavens, even if you fail, you will fall among the stars."

Fast forward nearly two decades. He had long since pulled his act together, gone back to school, and become an accomplished federal attorney. We covered a lot of ground over chicken sandwiches and Diet Cokes. I jerked his chain and told him I thought he would be a terrific writer. He jerked mine and told me he thought I would be a really good lawyer.

At the time, I was happily writing a novel. I also didn't think I had the brain power to possibly consider such a leap anyway. He wasn't buying it. He never had. "What, you think you're too old to change?" he shot back.

I went back home, mulled the challenge, and remembered that I had once long ago—before marriage and motherhood—even applied to law school when I was still a journalism student. I now took the entrance exam to see if my brain still worked, and found that, indeed, it did.

Something else entirely unpredictable was also at work in this equation. Between that lunch in Florida and the entrance exams, I had suffered a serious accident. Coming out of it still alive and still walking, I found I was even more determined to give this new path a try. And so I sent in my application to the only law school within driving distance, and was accepted. Eureka!

94

Three and a half years later, I graduated with an honors degree. In my early days as a law student, if I hit a rough patch, I reminded myself that John believed I could do this, shut my eyes, and forged ahead and did it. Eventually I came to believe more in myself, and didn't need anyone's faith to fall back on. But I was glad to have had it when I started.

And so I often tell my kids that kindness is never wasted. That if you have something good to say about someone, say it sooner rather than later, because you just never know what shores that encouragement will carry them to.

Just ask John. Or Cheryl. Or Aunt Patsy. Or me.

The Gatorade Reality Check

The Gatorade was officially labeled "Wild Berry," but it was a gorgeous, most un-berry-like deep azure blue. Like a swath of the Caribbean staring back at you from a glossy travel poster, beckoning you in the dead of winter to warmer climes with powdery white sand beaches, and fruity drinks with little umbrellas, and, just maybe, a cabana boy or two to ogle. Or those "blue raspberry" popsicles with the two sticks you bought at the corner store when you were a kid, racing to slurp them down on a steaming summer day before they melted and dripped blue stains all over your clothes.

Yes, the Gatorade was pretty under any other circumstances, but it was now pooling in the middle of a Laura Ashley bedspread, and my son's friend who had just spilled it entirely by accident in the room she was bunking in was sheepishly repeating "I'm sorry, I'm so sorry, I'm so sorry about this!" as I kicked into emergency mode and ripped the covers off the bed.

She was mortified, and I was scrambling, and my biggest priority at that exact instant was to keep this deluge of vivid blue from soaking through to the mattress. I made it by a whisker.

"Is there anything I can do?" she continued. "I'm so sorry, I've got another comforter along, I'm so sorry!"

I told her not to worry, and the young adults soon left to go out to dinner as planned. They threw the bedding into the back of my car for me, and I followed with a bottle of detergent and several bucks worth of quarters on my way to the Laundromat. And on the way there, in the cold and the dark, I reminded myself of what was really important in life, and why I didn't really give a rip about whether the very lovely comforter set was irrevocably ruined. It had already done what it needed to do.

I am not a person whose house has many luxury touches. My kitchen cabinets are made of the same particle board with plastic veneer that I moved my pots and pans into many years ago when we first built it. Half of the carpeting has been replaced—but the other half is still the original stuff, and shows every day of its age. The living room hasn't been painted in at least fifteen years. But one day I was seized by the need to buy a twin-sized Laura Ashley comforter and sheet set on the spot and bring it home.

The set is gorgeous. The comforter is a rich seafoam green and cream brocade, far too plump to ever fit in my own washing machine, ruched and quilted and heavy and…well…comforting. The coordinating sheets I bought to match are light shell pink, showered with pink cabbage roses in various stages of bloom and dark green leaves, evoking the carefree, mythic abandon of Marie Antoinette playing shepherdess at Versailles. And I bought them because my daughter had cancer.

She is completely, thankfully fine now, but life can change in a heartbeat. All of ours had changed a month earlier, when she called to say that she had been unexpectedly diagnosed with thyroid cancer.

Ten days before that I had been sitting on a tall stool in a crowded yuppie bar in the Twin Cities after midnight, a buzz on from the drinks had earlier in the evening. I was buying for both of my daughters and celebrating the older one's graduation from law school the next day. We felt like we had the world by the tail.

Less than two weeks later, I was getting ready to leave my office, peeling out of my spike heels, showing off pictures of the graduation ceremony to a friend in uniform, when my ex-husband called to tell me that my "training baby" had cancer. Bam, we entered a new universe.

A frenzy of shock and concern and activity followed, as doctors were auditioned and surgery was scheduled and insurance coverage was navigated. Work was rescheduled and plans were made to travel to the hospital and stay as long as any of us were needed. But before that, I hastily pulled together a graduation party for her (law school) and her younger brother (high school) on the only weekend before the surgery that we could all get together as a family. And if she was coming home, she was going to need a place to settle in for a few days.

This was no small task. She had lived away from home for most of the preceding seven years, while working on her undergraduate degree and then during law school. Over the past year I had turned her tiny bedroom—large enough for a desk and a dresser and a twin bed but nothing more—into a storage closet after the divorce as I dug out the master bedroom, repainted, hung lace curtains, reorganized. It took me three days to just get the extra stuff out of her room and move it temporarily back into mine, then dust and vacuum the room from top to bottom. And handle a last-minute felony drunk-driving trial as well.

And then I went shopping. It wasn't a rational, planned, shop-the-sales-and-just-be-practical kind of trip. It was a visceral, instinctive, primordial drive fueled by the thought that my baby was in trouble, and she needed a soft nest to land. And the Laura Ashley bed set was just the thing. The room looked stunning when I got done, far nicer than when she had ever lived at home.

We spent the next three days squeezing in as much togetherness as we could. We went to dinner, we went shoe shopping, we had the graduation party complete with a festive cake from the best bakery in town. We ate cheeseburgers and onion rings and sundaes outdoors at the local custard stand. I baked banana muffins, made coffee, got out fresh towels, hovered. She slept late all three days, burrowing like a mole into those pretty flowered sheets and brocade coverlet. And then, as the weekend came to a close, she went back to the Twin Cities to get the rest of her work and surgery arrangements in order, and I finally sat down and let myself fall apart. My friend Karin picked that exact moment to call out of the blue. When I heard her bright, comforting voice traveling through space, I cried so hard I was incoherent.

The Laura Ashley set is now back on the bed, all traces of Gatorade washed down the drain at the Laundromat, ready for the next houseguest. I was quite surprised. I thought that Caribbean ocean blue was set for the long haul, just another small reminder that life never goes smoothly, and if you expect that it will, boy are you in for some rude awakenings.

But if it had, I wouldn't have blinked an eye.

The Carpe Diem Girls

The Mississippi River rolled smoothly beneath us as we leaned on the railing of the cruise boat, resting on our elbows, facing into the light breeze. My daughters and I were soaking up the tranquility of the warm evening, the last of Indian Summer, like contented sponges.

The strains of live bluegrass music floated forward from a small group of musicians in the enclosed rear section of the deck. We were enjoying what we thought of as the best seats on the boat, right up front, with no one else standing between us and the river as we slowly cut our swath through sultry, languid side channels and into the river main.

We laughed as we passed a bottle of white wine between us. We had bought it earlier that day at a winery across the river in Iowa. Instead of fancy stemware, we poured it into paper cups scrounged from our bed and breakfast. And we acknowledged, though briefly, that we each had our reasons for looking at life a little differently now, as a lot more precious and finite and precarious, as "before and after."

101

My own moment of reckoning had come more than a decade before, though at the exact moment it happened I was too preoccupied with surviving it to look at the deeper ramifications.

Only two months after the "Superman" actor Christopher Reeve had been paralyzed from the neck down in a horseback riding accident, I took a long fall from a tall horse going over a jump and hit the ground, hard. My back hit first, then my head. I remember lying in the sandy dirt of the riding arena, blue skies and tree boughs above me, wondering when it would stop hurting enough for me to breathe again.

After some dickering and bickering and negotiating—I was sure I'd be "just fine"—an ambulance was called. I was strapped to a board, lifted in like a piece of lumber, and transported to a nearby hospital. I remember swapping horse stories on the ride down with one of the emergency medical technicians who had owned some Appaloosa horses. An exam and some paperwork and a CT scan later, doctors delivered the bad news. I had a broken back. A vertebra halfway down my spine had fractured. No, I wouldn't be going home that night.

I was shocked. Serious life-changing accidents were something that happened to other people, not to me.

In spent five days in a pain-killer induced haze in the hospital. Still, I remember some doctor explaining that it was too risky to try to stabilize the break surgically, so the plan would be to let it heal on its own. I was catheterized and confined to bed while the swelling in my back muscles subsided enough that I could finally be wrapped in fiberglass from collarbones to hips and sent home. Three months of aggravation, discomfort, and taking no deep breaths or showers ensued, followed by a good year or two of the kind of pain and weakness that even now still lingers.

It was a watershed for me. "Life is short, take chances, trust your instincts," were the top themes that rose to the top of the pile.

I had taken that fence a second time at the confident urging of my riding instructor, but against my better judgment and some strong argument from where I sat in the saddle.

"See, I told you so," seemed a churlish and petty way to view a grave situation, but I emerged with the indelible conviction to give that "inner voice" a much better hearing as well as a final say from now on. And to make the most out of every day I had left.

There was no rhyme or reason to luck, I knew, no sense at all to be made of the fact that after our equestrian accidents, Christopher Reeve was in a wheelchair and on a ventilator, and I was still driving the car pool to gymnastic practice.

And so I found my voice. I looked back at the fork in the road made fifteen years earlier—journalism or law—and gave the road less traveled a try. I got more accustomed to first recognizing, and then saying, "I want this. I *need* this." I went to law school, flourished like a flower in the desert suddenly blessed by a deluge, and picked a career in criminal prosecution.

And I was reminded every day, by the ache in my back, of how fragile we are.

My daughters have also had their own reasons for staring down the maw of mortality and coming away changed, valuing every shining moment. Anna Quindlen described this awakening well in her book "A Short Guide to a Happy Life," when she wrote about her mother's illness and death from ovarian cancer when Quindlen was only nineteen. We've each experienced what she called that "dividing line between seeing the world in black and white, and in Technicolor." The lights came on, she wrote, for "the darkest possible reason."

My daughters and I take little in the way of happiness for granted these days. And so after months of comparing our schedules, we booked a weekend for just the three of us to meet in the riverside town of Prairie du Chien, Wisconsin to do a whole lot of nothing...and anything else we could come up with.

For two and a half days we flew by the seat of our pants. We laughed and picked our way through a flea market in Iowa, ate chili and bison burgers at the Marquette Café, sampled wines at the Eagle's Landing winery, and shopped for antiques and candles and knickknacks at too many places to remember. Every once in a while we stopped to snack on apples we bought at a roadside stand and a plastic tub of homemade apple dip made of cream cheese, brown sugar, chopped peanuts and vanilla that I'd brought along. And we signed up for the sunset bluegrass cruise down the Mississippi.

The cruise was heavenly, the music wonderful, the evening temperature perfect as the sun dropped lower in the sky. As we gazed, and drank, and admired, one of the musicians took a little while to recount spending a few weeks in the mountains with his son—they were in New Mexico, I think—as they camped in rudimentary conditions and watched hawks together. It was a shared passion for them. He spoke warmly, and fondly, and eloquently of time with his son in soaring, splendid surroundings, of beautiful skies and cold nights and meals cooked on a camp stove.

I never turned around. Just thought, "oh, that's sweet...now how about another song?" My younger daughter, Sarah, bought one of their CDs at the end of the cruise, and read us the liner notes as we meandered around after breakfast the next day.

The next morning, our last, we crossed over the Mississippi River into Iowa again, to Effigy Mounds National Monument. We hoped to find a scenic hiking trail that wouldn't leave us exhausted. The day once again was gorgeous—warm and sunny, with a light breeze. The parking lot was packed, filled with families and other birdwatchers gathered to view the annual hawk migration taking place. A bald eagle flew above us as we walked from the parking lot to the visitor center.

A large white tent was set up nearby for T-shirt sales and music CDs. A small sign announced that the proceeds from the T-shirt sale would be going to support the family of somebody or other. The name rankled slightly in my memory. We looked the T-shirts over, and then started examining the CDs. Sarah stood at my elbow. "Hey, wait a minute," I asked. "Isn't that the same name as those guys on the boat from last night?" She wasn't sure.

I walked to another part of the tent. There was a newspaper article on display, a long and moving tribute to a young musician and his three-year-old son who had died recently in a car accident. It spoke richly of his family, and of his father, also a musician and fellow environmentalist and hawk fancier.

And a sad chill spread through me as I thought of the mid-music narrative from the night before, that fond reminiscence by a father about spending irreplaceable time in the mountains with his son. How he could speak at all amidst grief so deep was beyond me. And it reminded me once again of just how quickly life can turn on a dime, and that opportunities to say "I love you" should never be passed over.

We left the tent and found a trail that took us, panting in the heat, to the top of the bluffs. We had a picturesque view, looking over the glittering river far below that we had skimmed over just the night before.

Once we walked back down the trail, we knew, the weekend together would be over. There would be hugs and kisses and waves goodbye through car windows, but we each had a hundred miles or more ahead of us, and a return to the daily grind and responsibilities. We lingered, dappled by the sunlight that sparkled through the tree branches, feeling the wind in our hair, and congratulating ourselves for making it this far.

If we had the ability to change the past, I'm sure that each of us would summon a magic wand to undo the things that gave us such an appreciation that time is fleeting, and that life is fragile, and that beauty is everywhere and often found in small things.

But of course we can't. All we can do is gratefully wake up every morning, and think...*carpe diem*.

End of the Trail

It was not the kind of day I would have picked if I had the choice to make. In a perfect world, we would still have been at home, in a grassy field, with sunlight and warmth, and a light breeze riffling the pasture grass around us. There would have been wide open space, and a big blue sky, and a few more mouthfuls of tender green shoots to tear from the ground and savor.

But it was winter, and I had driven through a blizzard to get to the barn north of town where my two horses had spent the colder months for nearly twenty years. The snow on the unplowed road was easily as deep as the undercarriage of my Subaru. The wind rattled the big barn door behind me, and the snow drove sideways loudly into the metal cladding as the mare reached eagerly for another piece of sliced apple. I had brought a full bag. I didn't think we'd run out. It was time that was running out instead.

I had had at least one horse in my life since I was sixteen years old. That's when Hoki arrived as a frisky, untrained six-month-old colt. Hoki finally passed on the year before this, frail, most likely senile, and thirty-three years old, after a life spent mostly eating, sleeping, and daydreaming whatever horses dream about. Probably clover blossoms and a soft, warm place to lie down for a nap.

We had had some grand times when we were both quite a bit younger. Babe had made it a pair a few years after that, bought on a whim by my parents and ultimately transferred over to me. I joked often than their only real purpose in life was to be big, expensive lawn ornaments. And I loved to just look at them.

For the past twenty years that the horses spent the warmer months pastured at my house, I had been up at dawn and sometimes earlier every spring and summer and early fall day. I was often still in my pajamas, sometimes working by flashlight, measuring out horse feed and lately medications, and opening pasture fences. I don't think I will be taking note of nearly as many sunrises from now on.

The other horse stabled in this small barn, bigger and stronger and, I suspect, meaner, tried to muscle her way into the bulk of the apples. I managed to hoard most of them for Babe anyway. A half-dozen prize-winning Dutch rabbits who shared the barn with the horses, their cages nestled by bales of fragrant hay, watched us warily as I parceled out the apple slices, and wept, and kept repeating the same words as I stroked her shaggy neck, "Baby, it's going to be okay. You're going to be okay." The vet would be there soon. But this time, instead of making things better, we were going to end them.

There was a good deal of irony to the fact that the end of the trail had finally arrived during the first serious blizzard of the season. For years, I had labeled Babe the "Calamity Jane" of the horse world—anything that could possibly medically go wrong with a horse inevitably did for her. In the years I had taken care of her, I had nursed her through multiple, near-fatal bouts with emphysema, laminitis, and colic. An autoimmune disorder left her prone to eye injuries, and they arrived like clockwork every summer for years. And after each disaster, she had bounced back, defying the odds and sometimes the dire predictions of the vet.

But this was different. She had suffered a knee injury earlier in the year, and while cortisone shots had eased her pain and difficulty for several months, the knee had now deteriorated beyond repair. Walking had become a painful ordeal. She had looked at me only days before with the same plaintive stare I had seen through so many other struggles, the unspoken plea, "make it better." And I knew this time that I could not.

On this day, she was thirty-two years old, which translated to about ninety-five in human years. And only three weeks before, at that miraculously old age, she was still staggeringly beautiful. She was a palomino, with languid, blonde, Marilyn Monroe looks. Golden coat and flaxen mane and tail. Big brown come-hither eyes fringed by ridiculously long blonde eyelashes. A curvaceous rump, and gorgeous legs. She was lazy as all get out, and I joked often that she was—like many horses—as dumb as a bag of hammers.

But when she startled, and her head flew up and her haunches coiled, ready for flight, her muscular neck arched, nostrils flaring, and ears perked forward toward imagined danger, she was still every little girl's fantasy of the absolutely perfect horse.

Now, she was dropping weight by the day. On this day, she was damp and bedraggled from the snow melting on her back, and it was clearly a struggle for her to move. The vet finally arrived, and pulled his Suburban full of gear up to the barn door. Because of the blizzard and the snow drifts piling up against the barn door, we would need to put her down outside the barn to give the hauler a better chance of reaching her later and carting her body away.

There was paperwork to sign, of course, as there always is for the big, hard decisions in life. And then some more apples, and a nice shot of really good, strong painkillers for the last walk through the barn door. She followed me, trusting, past the rabbits and over the threshold through the small side door, and we stepped unexpectedly into the sunlight.

For a short while, the snow had stopped, and the wind dropped, and the blue sky peeked through the clouds. We trudged through the glittering snow to the appointed place, and I cried some more as I held her halter fast, and stroked her face while the vet busied himself with his needle for the final task. Then the moment came, and she dropped like a stone into a soft, perfect blanket of untouched foot-deep powder. She never took another breath.

She was a trouper. And she was beautiful.

The Devil on Horseback

The price of admission to my own mind cost less than a Godiva chocolate bar.

The Indian Summer sun beat down radiantly on my bare shoulders as I picked my leisurely way through a massive flea market beside the Mississippi River in Iowa with my daughters. We were giddy fugitives from routine on that rare weekend together. Meandering and winnowing and pointing things out proved to be a bottomless well of amusement.

Hey, look at those Saint Bernard puppies lounging over there in the shade! Get a load of the cute Halloween yard decorations! What do think this weird metal utensil was used for fifty years ago? Should I buy this?

We turned over crockery and porcelain teacups, priced knick-knacks, pored over collections of used CDs, sniffed fragrant soaps, and eyeballed cheap jewelry. And as I casually glanced at a box of second-hand books, the past nearly bit me on the finger.

There, atop a stack of other unmemorable novels, was the key to my formative years—a "romantic suspense" novel by Victoria

112

Holt called "The Devil on Horseback." The original paper dust cover was still intact, though faded. Center stage was occupied by a wasp-waisted young, beautiful blond with long ringlets trailing from beneath a feathered blue bonnet the size of a Volkswagen Beetle. She was flanked by images of a booted, sneering nobleman (in a smaller but just as ridiculous feathered hat) astride a somber chestnut steed. A tumbrel full of doomed aristocrats was parked conveniently by a guillotine.

I flipped the cover open, and scanned the thumbnail description of the plot. There was the beautiful schoolmistress' daughter, caught by unkind circumstance between the worlds of education and aristocracy and the hired help, forced by fate to make do while a "dark and cruelly handsome" French count thought she was "just the kind of mistress he had to have."

A bright yellow sticker advertised a handwritten price of a dollar. I couldn't resist. I didn't counter, haggle, barter or quibble. This book, I had to have. Reading it, I thought, would be like stepping into a time machine.

The title was vaguely familiar, though I couldn't remember if I had actually read it before. But since I had devoured everything I could get my hands on by Victoria Holt decades earlier, I'd have bet good money I had.

I will be the first to confess that as a child, I did not play very well with others. There could be a thousand explanations for that, but we are going to skip them all here. Let's just say that I read my way through my childhood and leave it at that. Growing up on the northwest side of Chicago, I practically wore grooves in the pavement to the local library at Pulaski and North Avenues, especially in the summertime.

No sooner would I finish an armful of books—Greek mythology, Nancy Drew mysteries, everything the library had about horses, especially the entire Black Stallion series by Walter Farley—then off I trekked. Past the Woolworth five-and-dime, and the Tiffin movie theater, and the bowling alley, and the delicatessen that carried those boxes of delicious Dutch chocolates shaped like tiny wooden shoes—but still always smelled like smoked herring. My arms always ached from the load, returning one batch just to bring back another.

The window of my second story bedroom fronted on the street, and from the middle of my bed there in the afternoon light I retreated into a world of language and imagery, Homeric adventures and western canyons, mustangs and mysteries.

It didn't do much for my social life…but it gave me one hell of a vocabulary and—years later—great verbal scores on my college entrance exams.

Somewhere along the line, though, I outgrew my hunger for stories about teenaged sleuths and Smokey the Cow Horse, and turned avidly to a new genre, romantic suspense. Phyllis Whitney, Victoria Holt and Mary Stewart were my new must-read authors, and my imagination became steeped in tales of young and lovely heroines in difficult circumstances drawn to brooding, distant men who magically turned out alright at the end.

Given that my first two years of high school were spent in a sea of plaid jumpers at an all-girls Catholic prep school, sightings of actual males were somewhat sporadic, and these books provided a more sophisticated window into love, courtship, and happy endings.

Or so I thought.

Fast forward a few decades. Back from the weekend getaway, I wasted little time in finally cracking open a window to a younger, less complicated time. I curled up in bed with a light at my elbow one weekend, and a few pillows propped comfortably behind me. With the doors and windows locked and cat, dog and son soundly asleep, I began to read. But a journey that started with amused anticipation segued quickly into a dutiful slog through repeated disappointment, finishing at long last with a sense of acute nausea…and relief that it was over.

Good grief, I thought, what mind-warping tripe! What toxic influence had cast its malignant and formative shadow on such an impressionable young mind!

This was a knee jerk reaction, of course. Nobody reads romantic suspense to get a dose of reality—all the ormolu clocks and clattering horse-drawn carriages and borrowed evening finery would see to that.

But this was ridiculous. I could—if pressed—buy into the potential quandary faced by the milquetoast heroine Minella of choosing a loveless, if affectionate, marriage to the Lord of Derringham Manor, or the reckless and tempestuous life of being the mistress of the sneering, bad-mannered and still-married Comte Fontaine Delibes.

But for heaven's sake, did this woman never think outside the childish confines and fantasies of her own mind? Did it never occur to her to just ask someone a question point blank about their motives or their feelings? If someone threw a brick through the window of the chateau, wrapped in a menacing note...*did you think that maybe she'd just go tell somebody??*

Patience worn thin, I closed the cover and thought about what to do with this new revelation. The trash can seemed too...undignified, disrespectful of the past and the arduous journey to the present. Keeping it seemed...unthinkable. Giving it away to charity...well, that would be like donating poison to a food bank.

The book sat for weeks in a corner of the living room, as I left daily for work or other errands, paid the bills, toted the firewood, got the oil changed in my car. And then the skies parted, and the ending to this story became clear.

As evening fell after a day of working in the yard with my boyfriend and our chain saws, I stood at the edge of the bonfire. It blazed with the dusty and cobweb-covered scrap lumber I had pulled from the garage, and the mountains of brush we had cut and dragged from the edge of the driveway and raked into the crackling pile. The heat was a palpable, ominous force, smacking my face and my shins if I stepped just a little too close. But step forward I did anyway from time to time, to drag the smoking vines and branches from the edges back to the middle where they popped and hissed

116

before dissolving into ash. I felt exhausted, but triumphant as well—a primitive goddess of fire tending.

I had grown proud of my incremental post-divorce independence, and I stood surrounded by the fruits of my hitherto most unlikely labors—the tons of gravel moved, the paddock fences repaired, the mulch spread, the plants dug in, the branches trimmed, the shrubs taken down to the ground with a hand saw. And I stood in the shadow of the house where I had fixed the leaky toilet, patched and sanded and painted the bedroom, installed knobs and handles on the basement cabinets, and even managed—after six months of peering through murky darkness on the front stairs—to change the light bulb in the dreaded light fixture over the foyer.

I fetched the offending book from the house, and pitched it into the fire.

And as the sparks wafted upwards in the dark and the flames curled greedily around the pages, I sent the "devil" back home.

Gone Fishin'

My youngest son eased the SUV backward down the shallow mud slope, putting the wheels of the boat trailer a few feet into the water. The channel leading to the lake seemed not much wider than the row boat, and I stood a few feet to the side, out of the way and out of trouble. I was in thoroughly unfamiliar territory, both metaphorically and literally—I had absolutely no idea where we were. Not that it mattered, since for the next few hours, I was entirely in his hands. It had to happen someday.

We were there on the edge of his favorite lake, putting an aluminum rowboat into the water, at my suggestion. I had practically begged, in fact.

Fishing had taken hold of Robert with a vengeance this summer, coinciding with the triumph of getting his driver's license and being able to haul a boat and a trailer behind his small SUV. I had soon turned a little envious of his water-borne adventures with his high school buddies. Okay, the part about getting up at five in the morning for a good start did *not* hold any charm for me. But overhearing snatches of their conversation here and there, I formed the wistful impression of hours spent soaking in the grandeur of nature. There were sunrises, sunsets, loons, ducks, occasional fish caught and released, and moonlit excursions under star-studded skies that involved more relaxing and talking about life and politics than actually fishing. It all sounded heavenly.

And so I bugged him to take me fishing on one of the last mornings before school started up again. We set a date and hoped for good weather. At the appointed Mom-friendly hour, I drove up bearing bug spray, sunblock, and McDonald's breakfast sandwiches for the both of us. Then I climbed into the front passenger seat, and settled in for the ride. He had been busy already himself, industriously packing fishing rods, tackle boxes, a cooler full of drinks, nets, a carton of juicy nightcrawlers, and life jackets.

This was entirely his show. He competently pushed the boat off the trailer, parked the SUV, and held the boat steady for me to climb in. We poled our way off the mud bottom and down the side channel until the boat started to float on its own, then paddled through an ocean of shiny green lily pads fringed by rushes and tall grass. The last of the lily pads finally behind us, we floated out into wide open spaces.

Only a few feet deep, and tiny in comparison to other recreational lakes in our county, this pond nonetheless had rustic charm to spare. Only a few houses ringed its shoreline—nature reigned supreme. Too shallow for larger boats and "personal watercraft," too difficult for access for more than the true die-hards who didn't mind getting muddy to get there, this was a lake for those few who ***really*** treasured peace and quiet and, dare I say it, utter serenity.

Great blue herons, standing four feet tall on long, twig-like legs, spread their six-foot silver wings and floated along the perimeter of the lake, slow and measured wing-beats indicating no hurry, no worries. Their necks arched back in graceful S-curves, and narrow heads perched regally above their chests, long legs trailing behind like a ballerina's arabesque. Unseen but nearby, sandhill cranes clacked musically from the sidelines, and Canada geese passed, honking, overhead. A pair of ducks shot airborne across the lake, all speed and business, like turbo-charged Mini Coopers compared to the herons' languid touring cars.

Wind riffled the crystalline water's surface, and we passed over forests of strange vegetation below. Some plants curled upwards like submarine calla lilies, others sported riots of long, furry arms reaching upwards and crossways, like chenille yarn for fish and mermaids to fantastically knit. A damselfly perched casually on my knee, and I let him sit, undisturbed. The weather was perfect. It was sunny, with no clouds above us but a small handful scattered at the horizons. There was a light breeze, enough to both keep us cool and to move the boat, but not enough to rock it.

My son set me up with a casting rod, and started with the basics: an earthworm on a hook, with a plastic bobber attached higher on the line to let me know if a fish started to nibble. Later in the morning I graduated to an artificial lure, and left the bobber behind in favor of the thrill of the chase. He upgraded to a "buzz" lure himself, hoping to land a northern. I surprised my son—it's nice to still be able to do that every so often—by casting respectably from the get-go. All those hours I had spent training my horse years earlier, lightly cracking a long-handled whip to snap the air just behind his haunches as he walked and trotted in circles on the lunge line, were still good for something.

We sat, and drifted, and casted, and occasionally motored to new spots, and detangled our lines from the weeds they inevitably snagged in. We landed four feisty bass, two apiece. I marveled at how beautiful of a day we had lucked out with. And I marveled, too, at how lovely it is when the roles get reversed, and how I could sit back and enjoy the ride.

There is inevitably a tipping point—or there should be—when you look at the child you have raised from day one, through diapers and ear infections and teething and bruises and homework and late-night trips to the emergency room, piano recitals and back-to-school shopping and driver's education, and realize that they can do some stuff on their own.

For my older son, that moment came when he was eighteen and I flew to Germany to visit him for a weekend. He was spending several months there as a foreign exchange student. I not only spoke no German, I barely knew which end of the country he was living in. I had started listening to a "German for Dummies" CD in the airport lounge before takeoff from Chicago, then gave it up twenty minutes later.

121

So for four days a few thousand miles from home, I took all of my cues from my son. He navigated the trains, gave me a walking tour around the neighborhood and the town center, picked a café where we had coffee and ice cream, warned me to keep my purse closer to me when we sat so it would be out of pickpocket range, interpreted all the signs and directions and bathrooms and menus, and translated more than adequately at a gathering of my German cousins before we left.

For my oldest daughter—the "training baby" we mothers have the hardest time cutting the apron strings on—the moment came as I watched her speak to a crowd of about twenty-five hundred students from an auditorium stage at a convention that she helped to organize. For the younger daughter, it came at the end of a long day at the office, a hundred and fifty miles of driving, and an awards banquet where she had received a scholarship. I sat on the living room sofa of her new student apartment after the dinner, the "guest room" where I would sleep that night in comfort just ten feet away. Her cat watched warily from the sidelines, and my daughter kicked into maternal comfort mode. Let me get you a cup of tea, she suggested. Would I like to watch "Sex and the City?" I put my feet up on the coffee table and accepted my new place in the world. It felt good. And now it was time for my "caboose baby."

Three hours after Robert and I first poled and paddled our way out to the middle of the lake, it was time to make our way home. He expertly located the tiny break in the identical stands of tall grass rimming the lake, and navigated us back up the channel to the spot where we had left the car. Grunting and struggling mightily, he wrestled the boat—usually a two-man job—by inches on to the back end of the trailer. I stayed out of the way as he balanced on the trailer and manhandled the full load, then tentatively worked the winch at his direction when the time came.

Gear unloaded and boat safely strapped down, we slowly made our way home and back to reality and routine. "Thanks honey," I said. "This was just...beautiful!"

The school year has started, the house is again quiet, and autumn is settling in. A few sugar maples have started to brilliantly catch fire and drop their leaves already, signaling an encroaching end to long days spent outdoors in shorts and sandals. There is no more talk about the need to get up at five in the morning to get that boat in the water. I can already anticipate breaking out my snowshoes after a good blizzard this winter, and we haven't even had the first frost yet.

The march toward the dead of winter is inexorable, with fixtures of hot chocolate, snowdrifts, crackling fires and frosty windshields on the horizon. But no matter how cold it gets, and no matter how few hours of daylight we have for months on end, it won't take much to get my mind back in that boat.

If you see me with a far-off stare and a smile on my face this winter as the winds howl outside and the snowflakes fall like cotton, chances are...I've "gone fishin'."

123

Mink Recycling

I don't know where the mink stole originally came from, or who it had belonged to before it ended up in my godmother's closet. But there were a great many things in Aunt Mary's apartment that I had either walked past over the years while visiting or had never seen at all. And now that she had died, it was a little too late to ask.

Amber earrings? Probably from her trip to Russia. A commemorative glass nearly as old as I was from a Kentucky Derby? I grabbed that immediately as we took inventory of the things in her apartment, preparing for the inevitable estate sale that would follow her funeral. My aunt and I both loved horses. She paid for my first horseback riding lessons, in fact, and rode along.

There was a full-length fake lynx coat hanging in the hall closet. This, at least, I knew the provenance of. I had helped her buy that coat at an upscale shop in Wisconsin on a bitterly cold day two decades earlier. I hadn't seen her wear it in years.

But what on earth was my never-married, history teacher, maiden aunt doing with a mink stole?

As we sorted and vacuumed and displayed and scrubbed and polished in preparation for the sale, the mink came out of the shadows and into the daylight. It was soft and clean and in good condition, but had obviously changed hands several times. The name monogrammed into the lining didn't belong to anyone in the family, so I guessed that my mother or grandmother must have picked it up for a song at someone else's estate sale years before and brought it home "just in case."

In case of **what?** Perhaps Prince Charming would come calling with an invitation to the ball, and it paid to be prepared. But I have never lived in an income bracket where the words "I brought home a mink *anything* today" would fit in a conversation about shopping, and I can't think of anyone else in the family that applied to either.

So the mink got priced and tagged, and attractively staged where it would be noticed by the foot traffic between the dining room and the kitchen during the sale. A lot of things walked out of the house by the end of the day. Many of them were pieces of heavy furniture that we were glad to be rid of. But the mink was still hanging there at the end of business, plush and furry and forlorn, and looking completely out of place in a middle-class second-story apartment in Chicago. Even the fire-sale price slashing we did right at the end of the day didn't get it to move.

And so the mink stayed on the premises a while longer, far back in a closet, as most of the other remaining unsold clothing was donated to charity and the knickknacks were farmed out for sale on commission.

Hopelessly languishing out of its proper social bracket, the stole managed to combine the appearance of a haughty society matron in humble surroundings, with the touchable, comforting feel of Lassie. A few months later, when my German cousin and her husband came to Chicago to visit, we had a family gathering of music and reminiscence at my mother's apartment, and somehow the mink stole came out for an impromptu modeling session. Nobody jumped at it even then. And so I finally brought it home with me to Wisconsin, where it took up an entirely new languishing position in the back of *my* closet.

Well, Prince Charming didn't come calling in a carriage with an invite to dinner at the castle. But a friend of mine who actually owns a set of white tie and tails invited me to a Viennese Ball. I had attended the ball for the first time just the year before, with the man in my life on my arm in a rented tux and a pearl tie tack, and we'd enjoyed ourselves enough to make a second appearance a done deal.

The weather that first time had been absolutely balmy, but this time the forecast called for snow snowers and temperatures in the low thirties that night. Really, what's a woman in a strapless gown and opera length gloves who's channeling her inner Hapsburg empress to use for a wrap?

Out came the mink from the back of the closet.

Now, I am not a "real fur" person at all. Many years ago, my first dog, Muttsie, got her foot caught in a leg-hold trap while we walked in the woods near a river. By the time I freed my dog's leg from that trap, there was blood on both of us. Something like that stays with you. Since then, I've had a knee-jerk reaction to the idea of fur coats and fur stoles and anything that involves killing an animal and displaying its pelt simply for status and fashion.

Aunt Mary was an animal lover too. I remember that we were both *very* pleased when we found that fake lynx coat during our shopping expedition.

On the other hand, I reasoned as I worked on my outfit for the Viennese Ball this time, I was doing a lot more recycling these days in general. More cardboard and paper, more plastic, more metal, more styrofoam. In fact, my "recyclables" usually outweigh the trash from my house.

And, I reasoned, the minks that made up this stole probably died at least sixty years ago. It's not like they were part of any viable stream of commerce after the Kennedy administration.

So...the mink came with me to the ball.

My transportation for the evening was a tiny Chevy Aveo with a stick shift, not a carriage pulled by a pair of high-stepping Hackneys. My date still wore a rented tux. I recycled the opera gloves from last year, and rummaged through my jewelry until I found a pair of rhinestone and faux sapphire earrings that I've had for a good fifteen years with *no* idea where they came from.

127

I bought a sequinned evening purse at a second-hand shop, and found a clearance-priced dress on a bridal website.

Oh, that mink stole put such a spring in my step! It was so soft. It was so plush. Wearing it was ***so much fun!!***

There's an older gentleman with magnificent mutton chop whiskers who attends this ball every year, dressed up in character as the 19th century Austrian Emperor Franz Josef. We have a lot of sport with the fact that in German, my name is "Maria Theresa," who was the only female ruler of the Hapsburg Empire. The first year we met he kissed my hand and sang "Lili Marlene" to me *a cappella.* I don't know if it was the mink or the rhinestone tiara or the architectural underpinnings from Victoria's Secret, but when we met this year he said with a twinkle in his eye that I reminded him more of Franz Joseph's mistress than the stodgy Austrian empress.

The mink has moved from the back of my closet to a spot closer to the middle, where I can see it and even take it out and pet it more often...like Lassie. In a middle-class life that mostly revolves around getting to work, weeding the garden, shopping for groceries and changing the cat's litter box on a regular basis, the mink is never going to get a daily workout.

But...the next Viennese Ball is only a few months away.

And I know that along with the gloves, and the rhinestones, and the sequins, and the chandelier earrings, the mink stole from Aunt Mary's closet...and I...will have at least one more chance to shine.

The CatBird Returns

Meatball moved in a couple of days ago, a temporary gig until the end of the semester. He came supplied with a cat carrier and a bag of "senior" cat food, in the arms of my prodigal college student son who was home for a 24-hour stretch of TLC and laundry service before returning to campus.

My son's first official action upon returning home was to stretch out on the sunlit sofa in the living room and crash for three hours.

Meatball's first official action was to put Lucky, the puppy, on notice that he'd be missing an ear or an eye if he got too close. Lucky is part Border Collie, so he's pretty smart for a five-month-old. Rambunctious, but smart. He took the warning to heart and is keeping a three-foot radius from danger most of the time.

We are all making some adjustments here, but for now I'm still basking in the afterglow of kicking into "mommy gear" for an entire day. I cooked dinner—turkey tetrazzini—one of my son's favorites. I actually had the oven and three burners going on the stove at the same time.

This was no small feat. I use my stove so rarely these days that after last winter's holidays, a mouse moved in under the left rear burner. I thought that Smokey, the house cat who likes to stage death scenes of his kills for my enjoyment, would take care of business. But in the end Smokey stayed napping on the recliner rocker, and it came down to me and a "live trap" I picked up at Walmart and a dab of peanut butter. I caught the mouse about five minutes after I set it up under the burner.

After contemplating the frigid outdoor release options, I finally set the little guy loose in the garage with a handful of bird seed. He repaid my largesse by getting in to my car a few days later and drowning in my half-full bottle of Diet Coke. Yes, I know, one mouse looks much like another. But in my heart, I know that this was the same little guy who had thought outside the box for his kitchen living quarters.

I did laundry—five huge loads of T-shirts and socks and jeans—and folded it too. This, too, was no small feat, and these days is **completely** out of character for me.

I made pancakes from scratch for breakfast, and served them with "real" hot maple syrup. This, too, was also a departure. Back when I still had four kids around the breakfast table and everybody wanted waffles or French toast, I bought the kind of "maple-ish" breakfast syrup that comes out of a plastic squeeze bottle and costs a fraction of the genuine article.

And for the crowning piece of nostalgic motherhood, I produced two new "Looney Tunes" collections of cartoon DVDs to watch as we wolfed down our breakfasts while seating on the sofa. You just can't beat the classics.

I've always felt a bit of the "kill the fatted calf" thing going on when one of the kids has come home from college. It felt great. It felt deeply satisfying. It felt like being a retired firehorse suddenly getting back into harness.

And through it all, Meatball kept chirping away like a canary. Yes, "meow" has generally been the expected cat commentary throughout recorded human history. Meatball just comes with a more interesting vocal range. I don't know how else to describe it, but if you were listening from another room, you would think I had a pet bird in a cage in there. And his sinister, raspy purr is faintly, strangely, evocative of Peter Lorre in "Casablanca."

This wasn't Meatball's first trip home. He was the very definition of Christmas for me just a couple of years before.

Back then I was behind on everything because of simultaneous family disasters a hundred miles away that had started in early November with my mother's broken leg and gone downhill from there. I wrote no newsletters and sent no holiday cards. I baked exactly two small batches of Christmas cookies before the kids came home, hung no garland, left the crèche in the storage bin, looked for but never found the mistletoe ball.

When the kids came home for a few days over the holidays, they were the ones who hauled out the ornament boxes on Christmas Eve and made sure that at least **something** was hanging on the tree. They made merry as they rolled out and decorated the traditional butter cookies in truly demented ways while I sat, exhausted on the living room sofa.

But Christmas Day this time came and went as I drove solo on the Illinois Tollway to Chicago and back, making a round of two hospitals and a nursing home to keep an eye on things on the only day without snow in the entire week. I was not a happy camper.

I was feeling very "Grinchy" that morning as I pulled out of the driveway at eight in the morning. But then as I drove, the sunlight and the season and the fact that I am blessed with children I absolutely worship finally got to me, and I felt a spasm of generosity twitch in my heart that up until then still felt two sizes too small. A half hour into my drive, I called my older son, who at the age of twenty-one was most definitely still deep in slumber, and left him a voice mail.

Merry Christmas, honey, and *yes, you can bring the cat home*.

Simple words, but they masked a world of complexity.

Mike had adopted Meatball from an animal shelter and brought him home to his student apartment about eight months earlier, where the eight-year-old cat promptly became known for leaving his odorous "mark" on his master's clothing when feeling peeved or neglected. The problem seemed to have resolved itself by Christmas, but I was still wary.

There was a very large cat, Smokey, who already owned my house, and so I drew a line in the sand at my son's plaintive requests to bring Meatball home for the holidays. I was thrilled to death that Mike had a cat, since I always think that life is far better with pets. But two adult male cats who were strangers sharing space in the same house? I could foresee only disaster.

So Meatball stayed home alone at the apartment with a big bowl of cat food and a big bowl of water while the rest of the family gathered and visited. And on Christmas Day, I wasn't going to be the only one on the road—my son planned to drive eighty miles back to his apartment that day just to check on his pet.

And so during my own Christmas drive, thinking of my baby spending half of his day traveling back and forth just to make sure that a middle-aged cat was okay, I took a leap of faith and relented. And felt better for the rest of the day. Three days of feline togetherness passed with no accidents and no bloodshed and a new era dawned in terms of pet visitation. Meatball proved to be no-fuss houseguest with the mind of a simpleton and the peskiness of a two-year-old child.

Things got a little more complicated now as my son prepared to go back to school. You could tell that Meatball knew something important was in the works as my son carried baskets of laundry out to the car...but not the cat carrier. Meatball stood on the staircase, chirping, as I got my last, heartfelt good-bye hugs. Then there was a final pat for the cat from my son, and the household was suddenly minus one young man.

And so we are all adjusting. Meatball has taken to dogging my footsteps like a puppy, driving the **real** puppy in the house absolutely bonkers with jealousy. Smokey the cat, sensing that this new arrangement may last a while, has taken to dourly stalking around in an existential funk and curling his vast, furry bulk into an empty laundry basket as though it was his Fortress of Solitude. I can't bear to tell him that it doesn't make him invisible. Lucky the puppy is putting up with the topsy-turvy reality of seeing the new cat sampling his dog food. It must be a dominance thing on Meatball's part.

And if you close your eyes and imagine, once in a while you just might think there's a canary chirping in the other room.

Pelican Lessons

Everybody's got "the story."

For some folks—most famously Oprah—it's the "aha moment," that wonderful instant in the cosmos when a vital, incredibly important, life-changing realization strikes, and the heavens part, the world divides into "before" and "after," and the path ahead becomes suddenly clear.

Before the "aha moment" entered the modern lexicon, it was the "Eureka moment." This of course stems from Archimedes jumping out of his bathtub a couple of millenia ago and running naked down the street with excitement at figuring out the concept of water displacement, which was a very big deal.

Well, "aha" and "Eureka" moments are great and all, but there's something beatific and divine and let's face it, even bland and rather undramatic about them in the long run. I think "aha," and I think of celestial energy and light flowing down from the heavens to shed enlightenment without irritation or effort or sweat or rueful discovery.

The story I'm sure everyone has lurking in their past and marking another important fork in the road has a bit more of an edge, and a definite learning curve to it.

This would be the *"I knew it!!"* moment. It's that flash of genius when you realize that you've been listening to the wrong voices (sometimes your own), ignoring your own insight and intuition, and turning a blind eye to the truth. It's that moment when a wife discovers her husband **was** in fact cheating, and the lipstick on his collar really wasn't hers; that the good advice of friends wasn't nearly as good as it seemed; and that the little old lady down the lane really **was** running the drug ring you suspected but just could never put your finger on why, despite the comforting smell of her gingerbread cookies.

The "I knew it!!" moment sometimes come with a tinge of regret, often comes with a "once bitten, twice shy" resonance, and always comes with the conviction that listening to your inner voice is the most important counsel you will keep from now on. It can appear while you're laughing out loud, crying with disappointment, or having coffee and croissants with a friend. And despite our avowed best intentions of listening to that inner voice from now on, if we're slow learners…we may even have more than just one.

In my own case, I'll admit to being denser than a gourmet cheesecake at times and so I have several of these markers along the way. The most portentious, serious, "high stakes" incident involved ignoring that inner voice in favor of taking one more run at a wood fence on a tall horse against my better judgment. It ended with an ambulance ride, lights and sirens, a back board, a great deal of pain, and the words "you have a broken back" to ponder for the next three months in a body cast.

But I'd rather not use that painful and traumatic reference point most of the time, when all I really need to think of are...*pelicans*.

The road to revelation was a two-lane ribbon of asphalt that ran through the Horicon Marsh. I was passing through on a long drive from the courthouse where I work to the university where my daughter was receiving an award of some sort that came with a fancy dinner. With no time to spare, no binoculars or birding guide in the car, and no hiking clothes either, I still stole ten whole minutes to explore a three-mile driving loop through the marsh that caught my attention as I neared. So I'd rather watch birds sometimes than talk to people. Sue me!

I drove deep into the marsh and far from passing traffic, and parked the car by a boardwalk that ran directly into the marsh. I stepped into a world of water and nature and trilling sounds and wonder. As the late afternoon sun shimmered on the water and illuminated the tall vegetation beyond, there were myriad takeoffs and landings around me, splashings and wingbeats and fluttering sounds. Something white caught my eye, and I stared in wonder as three huge white birds soared in from the periphery and came in for a landing past where the glimmering plane of water was interrupted by rushes and cattails.

I stood, mesmerized, until they disappeared. The golden sunlight gleamed on their outstretched white wings with the tips an inky black. From my far-off vantage point, I still could recognize a joy and an ease and a lilt to their flight as they circled and floated and finally landed gracefully in the reeds, well protected from prying eyes. These birds were huge. They seemed the size of hang-gliders. They were easily the biggest birds I'd ever seen.

And there was a flash of something familiar to them. For just an instant, I thought "pelicans!!" And then reason and rationality set in and I shut that thought down. "Nah," I thought. "Couldn't be." They were too big by far, entirely wrong in color, and a thousand miles from the Georgia shoreline where I usually saw them skimming the waves and the palm trees like prehistoric throwbacks, before alighting by the dozens on a sandbar in the Atlantic.

I got back in the car, drove the rest of the way to the awards dinner, and wondered all night and for days after about what exactly I had seen.

Could they possibly be whooping cranes? I knew that a few of these rare birds had been sighted recently somewhere in the marsh, and that seeing them was like finding the birdwatcher's Holy Grail. Could I have been among the chosen few?

I pondered the mystery for the next few weeks. I called a Department of Natural Resources warden I work with on occasion and asked his advice. Where had I seen this trio, he asked. We weren't entirely sure that the type of vegetation was a customary place for whooping cranes to nest. Had I thought about the possibilities of trumpeter swans, he wondered. And what about herons?

I stewed over the puzzle for weeks, reaching out to other birdwatchers with little satisfaction. The optimist in me really hoped that I'd seen a trio of whooping cranes. What an accomplishment!! What bragging rights!! But as I thumbed through my well-worn bird guides, I realized that this couldn't be the answer.

Whooping cranes would have the same silhouette in flight as the slightly smaller sandhill cranes I could identify in my sleep—a vaguely alien form, as though you took a goose and added an element of elastic to it, neck strangely thin and elongated, with long legs trailing out behind like twigs. I had caught just a fragmentary glimpse, but there was an elegance of movement that could not be denied. Just like a few bars of Beethoven's Für Elise can be mistaken for nothing else.

Likewise for herons—the size was off by a lot. The birds I had seen were enormous. And the more I looked at the descriptions and listings for trumpeter swans, the more I recognized that the flight pattern was wrong here too. The white birds I had seen soared and glided. They flew with a playfulness that swans and geese, I knew, just didn't have. If you've ever paid attention to a goose in flight, you know that it is a big-ass bird. That's a lot of meat to haul from one point to the next, and there's no room in that equation for burning fuel to have fun. A goose reminds me of a C-130 transport plane—it moves a lot of weight, and flies in a no-frills straight line.

I had reached a dead end. The mystery was still alive and well, but I was all out of leads. I tried to push it out of my mind.

A few weeks later, though, I was back at the marsh, this time for a leisurely morning of hiking and bird watching, a sanity break in a busy life, a battery recharge at the font of nature. With sneakers on and binoculars looped around my neck, I walked, and I sat, and I kept an eye out for another glimpse of those white visitors. Still no luck.

As I finally called it a day, I took a different route home, one that ran past the wildlife refuge's main visitor center. I stopped in and looked around. Then I stepped out on the deck and looked at the marsh spread out before me. A ranger was working in the office, and I put the puzzle to her. I explained the inspiring thrill of the sighting, the inquiries, the ponderings, the frustration.

"I'll bet they're white pelicans," she said.

WHAT!!!

Unbeknownst to my local ranger at least fifty miles east, the Horicon Marsh is famous as a summer breeding ground for thousands of white pelicans. I hadn't even known they existed. I had simply asked the wrong person for advice.

The ranger showed me a postcard with white pelicans on it in the gift shop. Sure enough, these birds looked exactly right. I ripped through my bird guides to the page on white pelicans that I'd never noticed, and there they were, in black and white and full color. With a wingspread of nine feet, no **_wonder_** I'd thought they were the biggest damn birds I'd ever seen.

And with that, I smiled, even laughed a little. "I knew it!!" I thought in triumph.

And now as I blunder through every day since then full of judgment calls and leaps of faith and decisions great and small, if I need a little validation for the idea of trusting my gut, I just look back at a warm spring afternoon on a Wisconsin marsh, and think...

They were pelicans. _**I just knew it!!**_

Home Fires Burning

The fruits of my labor were going up in smoke. In fact, they couldn't burn fast enough to suit me.

My late ex-father-in-law, a good man still dear to my heart, was fond of saying that cutting firewood "warms you twice." Once from burning it in your fireplace, and once more from cutting it up in the first place.

With all due respect for age before beauty, I'd like to add to that list.

At the moment, I could say that I was feeling mighty warm in the sunshine as I lugged the neatly cut pieces of firewood—harvested from yet another dead tree the wind had knocked down in the front yard the night before—uphill in a wheelbarrow to the wood rack in the garage.

Later, I knew, I'd feel positively toasty if not blast-furnace **scorched** as I set a match to the pile of broken and splintered branches that comprised the leftover trash from the wind's handiwork and kept a watchful eye on the blaze, raking smouldering logs and sticks from the edges to the glowing center of the fire.

And last, there would be warmth of a different sort—the cockles of my heart feeling a glow of satisfaction as the horrible, thorn-covered, scratch-inducing, virally opportunistic trash trees I had personally cleared out hissed and popped and shrank to glowing ash. Viewed with clinical detachment, in the war of woman vs. wilderness, the wilderness is winning.

But at this moment, the goddess of fire tending strikes again, at least momentarily prevailing in one skirmish in the ongoing war against forest succession that often takes the form of twisted, blood-drawing, spike-covered brush rivaling anything ominously guarding Sleeping Beauty's castle in a fairy tale. Fairy tales don't live here anymore.

I've come late to this primitive source of elemental amusement combined with necessity. With fifteen acres to keep tabs on, a good man with a gasoline-powered chain saw beside me, and a pint-sized chain saw of my own, I've been a fast learner.

One of the first rules of engagement is that, in the words of my Harley-riding Muse, "you can burn just about anything if you've got enough lighter fluid." And there are a few others, such as keep a hose nearby and turned on; don't leave the fire unattended. And then something I don't remember ever learning in Girl Scouts—if the wind is blowing in the direction of the house, close the windows before you get started!

143

But as with any utilitarian passion, there are graces notes that can elevate the gritty and necessary to the nearly sublime. A comfortable lawn chair, and a side table for a drink or two. Music makes the task better by a quantum leap—a radio plugged into a socket in the garage, a boom box if you're motivated enough to get up, strip off the work gloves and change the CD menu once in a while.

The binoculars usually come out as well. On this day, as the conflagration started to dwindle in the afternoon to more restful proportions, I sat and looked skyward.

A red-tailed hawk circled above the woods behind the garage, the afternoon sun gleaming off his chest and the underside of his wings. Turkey vultures rode thermals high above, their black and grey wings tipped upward like Vs, wing tips spread like fingers extended. A pair of Canada geese flew past, so near to the ground I could hear the "flut, flut, flut" of their wingbeats. A robin played tug-of-war with a worm on the far side of the yard. In the distance, someone fired up a chain saw and I smiled to myself.

Not all the burning going on at my place is just about cutting firewood and clearing out brush. There are days, like this one, when I burn down the past as well. After a quarter-century of marriage, I am still getting my bearings in doing things on my own, setting my own course, claiming my own space, owning my own heart.

Every piece of scrap lumber that I drag out of the garage and pitch into the flames feels like a celebration of moving forward. Of putting to rest a traditional division of duties and stifled suggestions, of the time when the garage was "the man zone" and I simply parked my car there, of when the kitchen was "the female zone" and my critical thinking skills regarding the house pretty much boiled down to making a better cake and picking out wallpaper.

Now I've got my own cordless drill and I'm not afraid to use it. If there's a leftover table leg or scrap two-by-four that I can't imagine a use for, pretty soon it will be up in flames. And while the fire licks greedily at its new, ephemeral source of power, I can feel not only the old patterns of the past going up in smoke, but any bad feelings too, lifted skyward on shimmering waves of heat and white smoke, to evaporate and then disappear.

I stepped away from the fire for a few minutes to walk through my garden, brand new the year before, savoring the promise of flowers where there had once been an austere, lackluster field of white gravel and weeds. There were signs of life even in the middle of April when the last of the five-foot-high snow piles melted to grayish bumps in the lingering pockets of shade.

Early-blooming Japanese peonies sent up red shoots on the south side of the house, inches from the last of the snow, promising intoxicating fragrance only a month away. There were buds on recently uncovered roses. There were coral bells, and tiny, fragrant sprigs of lavender. Foxgloves and holly hocks, sharp-bladed daylilies, irises, feverfew, daisies, all optimistically surged out of the earth despite the certainty that, in this part of the country, snow is surely just around the corner again.

I was burning solo this time. Two days of unseasonable near-seventies temperatures had driven me outside and away from the laundry and housework, out to the yard instead in leather work gloves and a tank top, wheelbarrow and hand saw and chain saw in arm's reach.

Bonfires in the past year have usually been a joint endeavor, a hot twist on what otherwise would be "date night" if we weren't too tired and grimy from all the yard work that created that "burn pile" in the first place. There's something intoxicating and deliciously warm about sharing a chore, a kiss and a drink, and a sense of total but tangible, worthwhile exhaustion earned with pure, hard, muscle-aching work. The "bonfire dates" have happened less often lately—a result of poor timing combined with snow, rain, cold, wind, and the schedules of our teenagers. But I know that the long, warm evenings of summer are just around the corner.

As afternoon segued into evening, my son returned from his weekend with his dad and sauntered across the yard. He finds watching a bonfire as mesmerizing and soothing as I do, and he quickly set to dragging more branches toward the fire pit and gathering armfuls of dead stalks that went up like tinder. We burned, and laughed, and talked, and caught up on the past couple of days.

Then as darkness fell, the fire died down to a pile of coals. I took the hose and sprayed the outer edges and grass surrounding the fire pit, and we headed indoors to make dinner and watch TV. Before we finally headed to bed, I went back outside and raked the pile of dwindling coals down once more, giving the smoking pile one more good drenching around the rim with the hose.

In the total cloaked darkness of night in the country, a few lone embers gave off a feeble red glow, as if to say they would not go quietly into that good night.

And it felt good to know that the home fires were burning.

Love in Wood and Wax

The words that made my heart leap, not to mention my adrenaline surge, weren't "I love you."

They were something more like "Watch it, she's coming down!"

I loosened the tension on the nylon rope in my leather-gloved hands, and quickly got out of the way of the forty-foot dead tree falling into my front yard. The man who inhabits many rooms in my heart had just notched the tree with his chain saw, and after a few more hours of hard and dirty work (mostly his, but I kept up my end by dragging shards and broken branches to the "burn pile") it would be turned into firewood to keep me warm the next winter.

My heart glowed…and not just because I was standing next to a bonfire.

I laugh these days at how my definition of romance has changed since I was in my twenties, and what meets the test for a token of affection.

Back in the day long ago when I knew much less about what I didn't know, the language of love followed a standard script, and the symbols were equally perfunctory. Flowers, of course. Candy, of course. Jewelry was always appreciated. Perfume...well that was more an individual choice, but it was the thought that counted. Oh, and don't forget dinner and a movie. The fancier and more expensive the restaurant, the bigger the thrill.

That was such a long time ago. Going off script has been so liberating!

The man in my life and I tally three ex-spouses and five children between us, along with three cats and a dog (all mine), and three small fish that live in a tiny aquarium on his kitchen island. There are jobs, and bills, and responsibilities, and run-of-the-mill irritations, and heartaches we could have never imagined when we were marching out the high school door in our caps and gowns.

But along the way, we learned to see ordinary things with new eyes, and feel much the richer for it.

That lesson hit me with the force of a hammer one summer day. My brand new car was still as shiny as a fresh copper penny when I was informed by my love that according to the manly code of car maintenance, it needed to be properly polished and waxed. I arched one eyebrow, but picked up a wet sponge and started slinging suds without demur. This is a man who owns not only his very own orbital buffer, he owns two.

Hours later, as midnight approached, he ruefully concluded that we had bitten off more than we could properly chew for the evening, and handed me the keys to his pickup truck for my drive to work the next day. He though he would have the job finished by the next evening.

When I drove back to his place a couple of days later, he was just finishing up. Even from a distance he looked exhausted. My approach was masked by the whirr of the shop vac as he whisked the last infinitesimal bits of dust from the car's interior.

I stared at the car, absolutely stunned. It gleamed like a sapphire in the sun, and I could see the knife-edged reflection of overhanging branches and the subtle shading of clouds above in its mirror finish. The car hadn't looked nearly this good when I drove it away from the showroom. I could put makeup on in its reflection.

I couldn't have been more moved if he had surprised me with a truckload of orchids and a pair of plane tickets to Hawaii. And therein was an awakening.

We don't feel compelled to follow much of the old script anymore. "Dinner and a movie" is often chicken breast or pork tenderloin grilled to perfection over charcoal in his back yard or mine, followed by a movie on DVD. Sometimes we go lowbrow, sometimes we shoot for an Oscar winner, and half the time we just fall asleep on the sofa halfway through the movie, too tired from the rest of the week to keep our eyes open past eleven.

I watch a lot more fireflies in the evenings. Viewed from the edge of the woods as twilight creeps in, they twinkle and gleam like sparkling gems on a dark sea, and there is a sense of mystery and surprise with every tiny light.

I get flowers often, cut from his garden, and they always make me smile. But even more, every day I step out into rose gardens flanking my front door that he planted and mulched when we were first starting to date. And as I walk along an Arizona sandstone footpath leading me through coneflowers and delphiniums and coreopsis and daylilies that replaced a field of crushed rock and plastic, I remember a shared experience of dirt and sweat and shredded cedar and digging, and think every day, "this is the garden that love built."

This year, I don't know if I'll be getting a box of fancy chocolate for Sweetest Day.

But I'm pretty sure that either in my fireplace or in a bonfire in the yard, we will be burning some of that firewood, watching the flames dance and the sparks float upwards in the dark.

And somehow that seems so much sweeter...and so much better.

The Vigil

The air streaming out of the grocery store cooler is dry and cold and bracing. I stand in front of an assortment of premium gourmet ice cream in single-serve cartons with high calorie counts and higher prices.

What flavor to buy for a dying man to coax him into taking a little more nourishment, a few more molecules of fat and sugar wrapped in the dulcet flavorings of Häagen-Dazs? Chocolate? He has quite the sweet tooth. Coffee? He loves his morning coffee. Dulce de Leche? Oh why the hell not? I buy two of each, then drive a few blocks further to a liquor store.

I am waging a war against death, and my pathetic weapons are ice cream, chocolate pudding and imported German beer.

It has been nearly a week since my eighty-six year old father, already afflicted by dementia and Parksinsons disease, was admitted to the emergency room for the second time in a month, with a perfect storm of converging handicaps—untreated diabetes, cardiac arrhythmia, a blood clot in his leg running from hip to knee, a raging bladder infection, and a grotesquely swollen foot caused by

152

circulatory problems. Unable to speak articulately for months before this, he was unable to tell anyone the things going wrong in his body this time until they had reached critical mass.

He has now made it more than three days past the phone call from the hospital telling me—as I stood at the counter of a German gift shop buying him more CDs of folk songs from his native land—that he would probably not live another half hour.

This old soldier is tough…but he is still wasting away. He is now in hospice care, a method of care designed to ease suffering rather than aggressively try to change nature's course. Treating him with something even as simple as an intravenous line for fluids and nutrition has been complicated by his dementia. He has spent most of the past month in hospital beds with restraints to keep him from tearing the IV lines from his arms.

A hospice worker who knows nothing of the man wondered aloud whether he had pulled his IV lines out because he wanted no further treatment to prolong his life. No, I retorted, given that he spent four years as a prisoner of war, three of them working as a virtual slave in a French coal mine, I think he was more likely simply trying to escape.

The conundrums are many. Enough pain killers and sedatives to dull the pain in his tortured foot keep him too sleepy to eat enough to regain some lost strength. Intravenous fluids would require readmitting him to a hospital and placing him in restraints again, which must be a horror to him. The difficulty he already has swallowing makes it more difficult to get any measurable amounts of food or liquid into his stomach.

And yet…I know I have made small inroads. A half cup of ice cream one day. A half bottle of German beer yesterday, a full twelve-ounce bottle this morning, sucked down through a straw while German soldier songs played on the boom box.

I knew I was on to something the day before when I lifted the straw to his lips and he tentatively drew in the amber liquid. Afraid that he might try to take too large a drink at one time, I pulled the straw away. He tried to speak, and I leaned closer to hear. It was just one word.

"Again."

Again what, daddy? More beer? Another single word answer.

"Beer." I look into his hazel eyes that still light up sometimes with recognition when he looks at me, and I know I will keep it coming. There is no "bar time" at this place.

I feel helpless to change the larger workings of fate, and so I focus on the smaller things that I *can* do. A promise to bring some Bitburger beer, an evening ritual from a family reunion in Germany a few years ago. The collection of German songs, which he sometimes taps his foot to or tries to sing along with. I remember to wear bright, colorful shirts, and perfume, and long dangling earrings to catch the light. My boyfriend, who speaks a little Deutsch from his time overseas in the Air Force, sat with us one evening and spun a tale of taking my father to Berlin to enjoy the next Oktoberfest. We set up a bird feeder on a shepherd's hook outside his window, and watched as goldfinches, bright as lemons, came to feed only minutes later.

I've brought my old dog, Bandit, to visit, tossing a bright yellow tennis ball around the hospice room to keep him busy. At one point I searched the room for the ball for another throw, but could not see it anywhere on the floor. It was only when I straightened up that I realized Bandit had placed it on my father's bed beside his elbow. I don't think my father knew this at all, but I still patted my retriever on the head in gratitude.

"You are *such* a good dog," I told him with feeling.

This evening as I leave the nursing home I feel an inevitability settling in, a waning of hope. The odds are long against him.

And yet, as long as my father is still breathing and still smiles at the sound of my voice, I will keep trying to fend off death, one spoonful of ice cream, one sip of Oktoberfest beer at a time.

Marsh Madness

The price of gas was nearly four dollars a gallon at the pump up the street, and the inevitable question to be asked before I turned the key in the ignition was, "is this trip really necessary?"

The sun was shining, and my good binoculars and weathered field guide to the "birds east of the Rockies" were in the passenger seat beside me. There was no shortage of stuff to do in and around the house on my day "off." I couldn't remember the last time I had sorted laundry. Papers—for work, for amusement, for health, for the kids, for taxes—kept multiplying in stacks every time I turned around and refused to file themselves. There were buttons to be sewn, dishes to be washed, socks to be sorted, dust bunnies to hunt down and exterminate.

And instead, I was heading out to the Horicon Marsh forty miles away to watch birds. Was this trip really necessary? Damn straight! Once in a while you just need to stop and take a "mental health" day away from routine. I eased the car down the driveway, and headed west, satisfaction and anticipation and guilty pleasure jostling for supremacy in my mind.

156

The first time I saw this extraordinary place, I was in a suit, and in a hurry. I was driving a hundred miles from the office after work to my daughter's scholarship dinner. A bailiff at the courthouse, well versed in both travel and transporting prisoners, gave me directions for the scenic route that would also help me avoid traffic delays. I drove along, already exhausted from a day that had started with opening pasture gates and measuring horse feed at 5:30 a.m., and then segued into hours in court.

I thought agreeably that the road less traveled was indeed scenic. And lovely. And repetitive. There's a lot of Wisconsin that looks very much alike. Red barns, green grass, black and white cows, wooden board fences weathered to a three-dimensional silver sheen.

And then all of a sudden I rounded a curve on a downward hill, and the enormous marsh spread out before me. It shimmered in the afternoon sun, water and vegetation merging and overlapping as far as the eye could see. The road cut straight through the marsh from east to west, a two-lane ribbon bisecting the marsh just above water level. Driving through had the feel of following Moses through the Red Sea. I spied a sign on the far side for an "auto loop," and took the bait. It was just a ten minute detour, and then I got back on track. I promised myself right then that I'd come back when I had more time to spend, and I have. I make the pilgrimage at least a couple of times a year.

On this particular morning, I was still seeing plenty of the same barns, and grass, and cows, and fences. But a bumper crop of spring dandelions cheerfully spread across the greenery like party favors. When I finally hit that straight stretch of highway flanked by water and big sky, pairs of geese casually herded their broods of olive-yellow goslings along the road shoulders. They must have parenting in high traffic zones down to a science, I thought, since the only road kill around were dead deer. Red-winged blackbirds perched on last season's cattails and flashed their scarlet epaulets, resembling unregenerate escapees from a military academy.

Driving into the marsh is like stepping out of time and into the meadow and forest primeval. From the time the car door opens you are enveloped by a symphony of bird calls in "surround sound," walls of joyous noise in a language we can't understand, but which communicate volumes anyway. Profusion is the key element, surrender the only path. Traffic noise falls far behind the deeper you drive and hike, until finally you are left with only the sound of branches bending, leaves rustling, and the occasional flutter and splash of wings on water, mysterious takeoffs and landings far different from ours.

Passing a side channel, I slowed to watch a sextet of painted turtles basking in the sunlight on a half-submerged log. Nearby, a blue-winged teal balanced motionless on one leg on another snag, his beak buried under his wing and his head almost hidden by his spotted chest.

I parked and took the boardwalk into the marsh, an incredible experience akin to "walking on water." I left my cell phone in the car, and slipped a camera into my jacket pocket instead. A Canada goose stood up from her mounded nest in the middle of the calm water, rearranged her eggs among the fluff surrounding them, and settled back down, her outstretched wings sealing in her warmth. Barn swallows and tree swallows swooped and dived, Mother Nature's versions of the F-15. A couple of American Coots bobbed their way down another side channel, with a slow, measured cadence like elderly beachcombers passing the morning at the shore.

The boardwalk gave way to a trail cut through the woods, and watching for birds gave way to a different kind of discovery. On this particular day, the forest floor was carpeted in white trilliums and purple and yellow violets, with a few wild geraniums in the mix. Fallen trees and branches, covered with moss, made for structural mystery in the distance.

The darkening sky looked like rain would be moving in soon, but I set out on yet another hiking trail, this one running through a meadow and some more woods. My favorite seat there has always been a solitary wood plank bench framed by trees and lilac bushes. Judging by the number of cars in the parking lot—two, if you counted mine—I was the lone human being for at least a half mile in any direction. I exercised my prerogative of solitude and stretched out on the bench, flat on my back. I took off my glasses, shut my eyes, and just listened. I was surrounded by a cacophony of warblers, sparrows, wrens, juncos, and who knew what else.

Can I identify birds by the sounds that they make? Almost never. I have a tin ear when it comes to bird calls. Can I even tell what I'm looking at without opening the field guide? Not very often, unless it's something that I've seen a dozen times before. But I can still marvel at just how much sound can some from such tiny instruments…and I got a kick out of the fact that one of my feathered troubadours today sounded a lot like R2-D2 in "Star Wars."

Picking up the pace as the clouds rolled in, I entered the woods again. I surprised a doe as I walked uphill and around a turn in the forest. We both startled, but with a few graceful leaps, her white tail upright like a flag, she was invisible in her element in seconds.

I reentered the car, and the modern world of technology, just as the raindrops began to hit the windshield. Still, I stopped often on the road to the exit, turned off the engine, and just watched through the open window. A female summer tanager, brilliant yellow and pale green, flew to and from her nest in the fork of a tree branch. Pairs of geese floated along with their goslings between them, disappearing into the forest of cattails standing in the water when they felt too much attention was being paid.

Four and a half hours had passed from the time I left the house until the time I got back, more than three of them "on the ground" at the marsh. The laundry still sat in baskets, the dinner plates still hadn't walked themselves into the dish washer, the cat had shed a half-dozen more fluff balls the size of small tarantulas around the living room, and the dog still looked at me with those sad eyes, telepathically communicating his reproach, "you don't spend enough time with me!" Never mind that "enough time" for this dog would be upwards of twenty-four hours a day.

But still, in the grand scheme of how to spend four hours if you don't have a gun to your head or a wolf at the door...was this trip *really necessary?*

You bet your ass.

Chocolate Sobriety

I made it forty-five days once. Forty-five days of grasping, white-knuckled determination, of denial, of yearning. Forty-five days of walking past the siren call of an unfinished Kit Kat candy bar on the kitchen table, of reaching for a pretzel instead of another Hershey Kiss.

Chocolate sobriety ain't for the faint of heart. The forty-five day stretch was a benchmark twenty years ago that hasn't been equaled since. Though I tried it again earlier this year, daring to think that even if I started not shortly before the "chocolate holiday" of Easter, I could hold my breath and tough it out. I should have known better.

I made it nineteen days this time, each day of denial meticulously marked off on a three-by-five card stuck to the refrigerator door, each day a badge of pride and punishment and self-control. I got derailed, this time not by the Easter Bunny but by my cousin Ann in Ireland, when she cheerfully welcomed me and my son to her lovely kitchen overlooking the Atlantic Ocean by opening a box of Irish chocolate-covered biscuits. When in

Rome, do as the Romans do. When in Dunmore East...well, the chocolate always **does** taste better in Europe.

We are talking hard-core addiction here. Whatever chocolate cake happens to be in the refrigerator after a birthday celebration is of course breakfast the next day. That holds true whether it's my sour-cream chocolate layer cake with buttercream frosting, chocolate covered mint squares, death-by-chocolate brownies, or chocolate amaretto cheesecake. I can eat chocolate for breakfast, lunch, dinner, and mid-day snacks. And frequently do.

I raid the candy bowl at work on a daily basis. If I haven't stopped by for some chocolate by ten in the morning, the secretary who fills it thinks something must have happened to me. I used to keep a stash of Dove chocolates in a another prosecutor's office down the hall on the theory that if they were in my desk they'd be gone in a few hours, but if they were stored in his file cabinet, I would be too embarrassed to make more than one or two raids a day. He retired a couple of years ago. I'm still feeling withdrawal pains over the end of our arrangement.

I knew I was in serious addiction territory years ago when I read a lengthy and serious article about alcoholism in a serious newsmagazine. It was the cover story, in fact. As I read through the checklist of warning signs, I realized that I could substitute "chocolate" for the word "alcohol" in each of the dozen red-flag questions designed to getting you to run for your life toward a recovery group.

And yes, I know the answer to the joke "Why are there no twelve-step programs for chocoholics?" Because nobody wants to quit.

It's not that I really don't want to, for many good reasons. The extra forty pounds I'm carrying, for one. All the cravings and the mood swings and blood sugar spikes and crashes for another. You can talk all you want about new medical findings that dark chocolate is actually good for your health. (And in fact, my cholesterol level and blood pressure are pretty darn good, thank you very much!) The fact is that I've been hooked since I was a little girl and my mother fed me Hershey Kisses as treats on the theory that all other candies containing artificial food colorings were bad. Chocolate is my comfort food, my "brain food" when I'm on a deadline, my preferred dessert, my ultimate self-indulgence. Give up sex or chocolate? Hmmmmmm....... gotta think about that one for a minute!

I still look back at that forty-five day stretch with longing, and pride, and ultimately disappointment. And I remember exactly what threw me off the wagon.

I had taken my four children to Chicago for a family visit around Easter time. They ranged in age from eleven down through one-and-a-half years old. Into the minivan went the kids, suitcases, collapsible stroller, diaper bag, snacks, toys, and books. It was like packing for the diaspora. And we then crammed a lot into a day that didn't go nearly as smoothly in real life as it had in the planning stages.

When we arrived, we unloaded some of the gear and replaced it with my Aunt Mary. We took off to visit the Museum of Science and Industry on Chicago's far south side. When we arrived, we found that the exhibit my aunt wanted us to see was closed. We then drove back toward the city and went to the Field Museum of Natural History instead. Parking lot renovations had us walking for blocks to get there. Then we waited for nearly a half hour in line to get our lunches at the crowded McDonald's in the museum basement. Holiday cheer with your fries, anyone? I rescheduled a get-together with a friend from college until later in the day because of all the hitches thus far.

Museum-going finally behind us, we tried beat the rush hour traffic on the interstate by taking the side roads out from the Loop. We got snarled instead in the giant traffic jam surrounding Wrigley Field for NBA star Michael Jordan's professional baseball debut in an exhibition game between the White Sox and the Chicago Cubs.

Exhausted and frayed, we finally dragged ourselves back to the house, and lugged the kids and all their gear up to my aunt's second story apartment. She reached behind her to the fireplace mantel, and took out some Easter treats that she had hidden behind some framed photos. They were from Fannie May, a Chicago institution and my favorite chocolate source since childhood. I had spent a college summer working in the Loop, never packing a sandwich. Instead I made a three-day lunch circuit between Fannie May for a quarter pound of chocolate; Baskin Robbins for a triple-scoop ice cream cone; and Heinemann's bakery for a couple of chocolate donuts. Aunt Mary had bought each of her grand-nieces and nephews a bag of Fannie May chocolate eggs and a Fannie May chocolate bunny, and she started handing them out.

"Gee, Mary Therese," she said. "It's such a shame that now's the time you've decided to give up eating chocolate." This wasn't a taunt, just an observation, but I felt something inside me snap. I looked down at Robert who was not quite two, and realized that he would have no memory of this moment. I turned to my aunt, and ordered, "Give me that bunny." It was gone in seconds.

That was the high point on the chocolate sobriety meter, or the low point, however you look at it. Although addiction has just now shown its better side.

I had some surgery done on an outpatient basis, and my good friend Judy came to the hospital to babysit me there and then take me home. Blessed with a nursing degree, a wicked sense of humor, and friendship of more than three decades, Judy came fully equipped with an apple ("an apple a day keeps the doctor away!"), a box of Garfield-decorated bandages, a gardening magazine, a box of chocolate-dipped devil's food donuts for my breakfast the next day, a bag of Dove dark chocolate miniatures, and a bag of Ghirardelli 60% cacao dark chocolate squares. This last would be chocolate of thoroughly medicinal strength if you believe the research these days. Not on the hospital menu, but still assuredly very, very good for you.

The operation went off without a hitch, though between the general anesthetic and then a shot of morphine for pain later, I was pretty out of it for a while. Still, after a half-hour of chewing on the ice chips that Judy was spoon-feeding me, I was starting to feel restless and ready to leave.

The thing about hospitals and nurses though, is that they want you to hit certain benchmarks before they let you leave with their blessing and a sheet of instructions in six-point type. Chewing ice chips is one. Not falling over when you get up is another. And proving that you can eat something without throwing it back up later is another key test. Okay, I played ball. "I want some sherbet," I said.

The order went out into the hospital universe somewhere. The patient wanted sherbet—not soup, not sandwiches, not cheesecake. More ice chips followed, along with an unassisted benchmark trip to the bathroom. There were more sips of water, and more ice chips. Where was my sherbet? It was somewhere in transit. I settled in yet again, watched the clock, watched Dr. Phil, ate some more ice chips, and got dressed in my street clothes. There was still no sherbet on the horizon.

The kitchen staff must have had to dispatch someone to go to the Himalayas to shoot the elusive Tibetan sherbet yak, and preparation was still ongoing. It was time to take matters into our own hands. "Judy," I said, "I think it's time we broke into the chocolate."

We hit the Ghirardelli chocolate first, and then the Dove. I kept it all down, although the "cotton mouth" effect of the anesthesia made it a little hard to swallow in the first place. Still, I performed well enough to impress the powers that be, and I was finally loaded into a wheelchair and pushed out to Judy's car waiting at the curb. The sherbet finally arrived as I was leaving.

I dug into the sherbet—now thoroughly unnecessary—as I was going through the sliding doors, and finished it as we drove down the street to my house. I was free, and I had Judy and the chocolate to thank.

Score one for my demons.

The Romeo and Juliet Song

There's a guilty pleasure I just have to confess. And then explain.

Not that there isn't already a list. Belgian chocolates. High heels. Coastal Georgia. Guys in uniform. The movie "Gladiator." Tropical drinks with little paper umbrellas. Down pillows and flannel sheets.

But this is a chapter, and a phenomenon, all its own.

I'm a grown woman over forty...and I like the Taylor Swift song "Love Story." There. I said it. Out loud.

You know the song. There was a time you couldn't possibly escape it on the radio. It's the one where she's Juliet and he's Romeo and it's got pre-feminist-to-the-point-of-Neanderthal lyrics like "Romeo save me..."

Good God, I thought, the first dozen times I heard it...or heard enough of it to wince and change the channel. How utterly *dopey!* How ridiculous. How unreal. How... god-awfully uncomplicated, and fairy-tale, and unconnected to the realities of love and relationships. And for heaven's sake, didn't she read to the end of Shakespeare's "Romeo and Juliet" and realize that the star-crossed lovers ***died??*** So much for teenage romance!

So that was the starting point of the journey to actual affection. Active dislike, morphing into something warmer. Just like real life. Or any number of romantic comedies, such as "You've Got Mail." Okay, Tom Hanks and Meg Ryan had a lot to do with making that one work. But still...it's a classic formula for romance on the big screen. Even Harrison Ford got to be loathed by Anne Heche in "Six Days Seven Nights"...and nobody doesn't like Harrison Ford.

It was the beat that caught me first. Rhythmic and pulsing and steady and smooth (relentless, even), like the slap of a plastic jump rope on a summer sidewalk. Three or four girls killing time on a warm afternoon, the jumper in the middle always switching out, the rhythm as consistent and steady as crickets chirping. Equilibrium as perfectly maintained—despite the occasional shift in positions—as a gyroscope spinning on a picnic table. I found myself humming along, even after I changed the channel. And then I quit changing the channel altogether, and looked at it through a new window.

Everything that drove me nuts about it at first—especially the cloying fairy-tale neediness of it—became a window into being a teenager again. Back in the day when all you could see was what you wanted, with all your heart, right ***now***, with no thought for the future other than the naïve believe that love could conquer all.

Remember those days? Mine, I'm sure, were fueled by a childhood spent reading too many romantic suspense novels full of dukes and other noblemen waiting to rescue their damsels in distress and whisk them off to a life of happily-ever-after. It took me years to outgrow that template.

Well, by the time you've passed thirty-nine, you've grown up and figured out that no matter how grand love may be, it doesn't always conquer all. It certainly doesn't get the toilet fixed, or the living room painted, or the dog taken to the vet. Real life is full of real frustrations, big and small, and tender euphoric feelings sometimes have to take a back seat while you run to the corner gas station to buy a carton of milk. Because you just can't live on love all the time...groceries and utilities and clean laundry and taxes are usually involved too.

But...

I finally realized that when I listen (and even...*ulp*...sing along to) "Love Story," I don't have to think about real life at all. It takes me right back to being sixteen and blissfully ignorant of the myriad disappointments and compromises that real life would bring later. By the time the song wraps up with "Romeo" on bended knee telling our heroine to go buy a wedding dress because he loves her and that's all he really knows...I get a quick fix of bottomless yearning fulfilled and a "when dreams come true" instant that's about as real as the Disney version of Cinderella, and just as much fun. Reality be damned. Just for a minute!

And, as I've learned, those magic moments aren't entirely lost when your teenage years are behind you. I had one of my own in the middle of a gardening project with a man whose pickup truck and leather tool belt and love of blooming things beat out any central casting figure of a prince on a white horse.

One Sunday morning, after the plants were in and the mulch was spread and green things were beginning to take root, the subject of putting in a footpath through the flower bed came up over coffee. I, cursed with deep character flaws of ambivalence and a pathological fear of commitment and absolutely no imaginary sense of the visual, balked at every suggested solution. Hedged, even, at the idea of going window shopping. For rocks.

But we took the truck out to a local quarry anyway, just for something to do. Between us, there was the fig leaf of understanding that there were always supplies for his own place that he could stock up on, and therefore this wouldn't be a trip wasted. We walked, hand in hand in the sunshine, over pretty displays of granite and marble and slate and bricks set into the walkway. And when we reached a stretch of red Arizona sandstone, I suddenly saw my heart's desire. And imagined it spread among my flowers.

I still hemmed and hawed, pricing it out, trying to figure what I could afford, balking at the enormity of the project, wondering whether I should go back home and think on it for a while longer. Like at least another week or two. And then Prince Charming cast his two cents into the pot and roughly rounded it up to the fact that this was exactly what I wanted, we had the truck with us, it was a gorgeous day, and we might as well just go for it.

I still remember the joy bursting in my heart as I threw my arms around him then and kissed him in the sunlight somewhere between the limestone and the crushed lava, casting all caution to the wind and simply saying "*yes!*"

As blissfully perfect and momentarily satisfying as the ending in "Love Story"?

You bet!

Objects in the Rear View Mirror

The news of his death was nearly four years old, but it was still news to me.

Earlier that day I had appeared in court for a routine set of "initial appearances" on some criminal cases, and had smiled to myself at how closely one of the defendant's names resembled that of a boy—a young man, really—I had been in journalism college with. It had been a good fifteen years since I heard from him in the aftermath of a college reunion only one of us attended, our brief updates changing hands via email.

He had become an acclaimed newspaper reporter in his field, and had gotten married, and back then he'd told me that and his wife were eagerly awaiting the adoption of a daughter from China. He sent me a copy of a recent award-winning series he'd written to bring me up to date on his work. I can't remember if I returned the favor.

I promised myself that I would look him up when I got home after work and send him a quick email about my morning in court for a shared laugh. But while I waited on "hold" as a polite, drawling young police officer in Alabama searched for some information about an individual I had charged closer to home, curiosity got the better of me and my fingers quickly typed his name on Google.

I hit the "enter" key with a quiet confidence, expecting to find the name of his most recent newspaper employer and, hopefully, an email address. What popped up on the screen instead was an obituary. And the news that his death nearly four years earlier had been "investigated as a suicide." My smile of anticipation turned to the taste of ashes.

Thirty years passed away in an instant, and I felt both hollow and tremendously sad.

My mind kept turning back to younger, more innocent days, when we all shared the shining idealism of young journalists in the post-Watergate era. Dustin Hoffman and Robert Redford had made investigative journalism seem not only rigorously principled but absolutely *glamorous* in the film version of "All the President's Men" just a couple of years before. Nobody told us we couldn't change the world every day, and even if they did, we wouldn't have believed them.

The young man I remembered was tall and slender, with gorgeous deep brown eyes and the broad shoulders of a swimmer. We were never very close, but our journalism school was small, and everybody pretty much knew everybody else. I remember that he was unfailingly polite, and well spoken, and ferociously smart.

He was a couple of years younger than I was, at a time in my life when things like that mattered, and he had what I think of as "Breck Girl" hair—layered and a bit stylishly long, and shiny and squeaky clean. He cooked dinner for me at his apartment one evening—one building over from where I lived with my roommate—and I remember a night of baked pork chops and candlelight and glasses of wine and nice conversation. We shared a G-rated kiss in his doorway as I left to go back to my own apartment and reality.

I printed off a bunch of pages about his passing. I took them down to the lakefront the next day, and read them in solitude under a cold, sunny sky. There were so many things I had not known. There were profound and well-earned accolades by the dozens, fond reminiscences, tributes to his inspiring and encouraging nature, celebrations of his colorful character and incredible intellect. But along the way there had evidently also been depression, professional turmoil, and a strange admission years earlier that he had slept for a while with a gun under his pillow.

The thing which had apparently tipped the balance for him to take his own life beside his favorite fishing spot, it was reported, was an upcoming initial appearance in court on a charge of drunk driving. The sort of thing that is absolutely routine for me on the other side of the table, but in his position obviously terrifying and unfathomable. I guess it's true that "the bigger they are, the harder they fall." I tried to put myself in his shoes, tried to imagine how he must have felt at this very public frailty, his reputation as a crusader for the public good on the verge of being seriously tarnished, and the humiliation that would have followed. It didn't feel good.

As the days passed, the shock finally lessened. I tried to "shake it off," rationalizing that we had never actually been close friends, that I shouldn't feel this so personally. By the next time I had to appear in court for more initial appearances in drunk driving cases, I was back to my usual form, confidently asking the court to require this, that, and the other thing as bond conditions "for the protection of the public." It's my job, it's what I do without hesitation and without doubt.

But in the moments in my office when the phone isn't ringing, when nobody's looking for my signature in a hurry, and I've caught up just briefly with the tide of paper that drives my work, I can see him still.

Tall, slender, in blue jeans and a checked shirt, standing at the top of the stairs outside his apartment, smiling at me as I left, his eyes a beautiful brown, and the light from the hallway shining on his fluffy "Breck Girl" hair.

Bunny Blues

I miss the Easter Bunny.

To be perfectly precise, I miss *being* the Easter Bunny. And Santa Claus. And the Tooth Fairy. I miss the whole "Masterpiece Easter Theater" and "Masterpiece Christmas Theater" quality of it all, the behind-the-scenes planning, the skullduggery, the hiding places, the fear of being found out. But most of all I just miss being the Easter Bunny.

To be perfectly candid, being the Tooth Fairy just couldn't compare for emotional payback. Two minutes of "oh look what the Tooth Fairy left me" was a paltry reward to balance out the fear of discovery as I tiptoed into dark bedrooms to make the tooth-for-money swap, circles under my eyes the next morning from staying up long enough to make sure the kid was asleep, and the overarching anxiety worrying that I would fall asleep and forget to play my crucial part. In fact, I *did* forget once. Egad!!! But I covered the lapse by going back to my daughter's bedroom to search one more time, and accidentally "found" the dollar that had "fallen" between the bed and the wall. Good save, eh?

Christmas with little children in the house, on the other hand, was the Sistine Chapel of maternal deception and orchestration, the prime example of why I have long said that one of the qualities of being a really good mother is the ability to lie like a rug. It requires approximately two months of planning, shopping, hiding, wrapping and decorating and, closer to the big day, ornament hanging and cookie baking and "Secret Santa" shopping for school buddies and last minute presents for teachers. But the rewards? Absolutely acres and acres of emotional recompense. Just feel the warmth of that crackling fire! Watch the tinsel on the tree glitter and gleam by candlelight! Hear the squeals of excitement at seeing what Santa brought while they were sleeping—in exchange for a time commitment akin to planning the Normandy invasion.

But Easter, ah! What a lovely change of pace! Religious origins and overtones aside, it is a holiday devoted in great part to the pursuit of chocolate bunnies and chocolate eggs and jelly beans, and the riotous fun to be had when a half dozen people sit around the kitchen table trying to outdo each other dyeing and decorating hard-boiled eggs. Pastel plaid has always been my favorite.

With my youngest now married, I have not had any true believers around the house for quite a while. Although for several years *after* this caboose baby finally wised up, we still went through the motions of hiding Easter baskets and plastic eggs full of goodies. The image of college kids in their pajamas running around the yard in the snow and laughing, looking for plastic eggs under bushes on Easter morning, will *always* stay with me!

To my credit, my youngest actually made it to the age of ten before I finally lowered the reality boom. It was tempting to see how long I could keep up the fantasy, since his older siblings were all still gamely in on the deal. But the day after Easter that fateful year was followed by his first day of baseball practice. I imagined him showing up on the playing field that day, happily telling about "what the Easter Bunny left for me!" And then the older guys on the team would just eat him alive.

So, reluctantly, I took a deep breath that Monday morning, steeled myself, and fessed up. I was the Easter Bunny. And the Tooth Fairy too. He seemed to take the news in stride and walked off. But he came back a few minutes later as I was fixing my hair in the bathroom, and his eyes were wary.

"You'd better not be Santa Claus too!" *Oooooooohhhhhh*, now the jig was really up.

For roughly the next six months, even longer, I could see that his trusting, happy universe had shifted to absorb the magnitude of the truth and the scope of the life-long trickery. He would hold up a favorite toy, a game, a book, with a mixture of discovery and reproach.

"So this came from you and not from Santa Claus?" Huh. Maturity is a hard thing to watch evolve. Although the following year he didn't let his newfound enlightenment interfere with his glee at decorating eggs again, or searching for his Easter basket before church started, or combing through the yard with the older kids for his share of the treats hidden there.

180

Easter has lately become far more subdued, the Easter Bunny noticeably absent. One year I took the boys to Germany with my father over the Easter break. The year before that had been the "year of the divorce" and entirely new arrangements. Yet another Easter passed with me and my youngest son in Ireland, traveling for a week and visiting with my cousins. I filled the usual baskets with chocolate and then left them behind. The action felt quite hollow.

And to make matters worse... Children living away from home and over the age of being hoodwinked are one thing, but even the pets have taken their toll on the holiday.

The centerpiece of my Easter decorating had long been my "Easter tree." This spindly artifice traditionally sat in the center of the living room's bay window. From its myriad branches hung fragile eggs I had personally blown the contents out of and then hand-painted back in the day when I baked a lot more cookies and read bed-time stories and still watched "Sesame Street" at lunch. The painted eggs were adorable, if I must say so myself. There were scenes of grazing sheep on one, a mallard duck wearing a tie and carrying a briefcase on another, and a mother duck with a beribboned bonnet and four ducklings on yet another.

I haven't brought the Easter tree out of hiding since we brought Smokey home as a tiny kitten. I've seen what that demented maniac does with Christmas tinsel. And a new wrinkle was added when the dog came late to the realization that the bay window sill is a fine place from which to stand and bark at the world when I'm not at home to chase him off.

Life is very good right now, even though none of the Easter toys or decorations have come out of the box for years. I have a marvelous new grandson. All the kids and I will get to happily reconnect at my nephew's wedding soon, and share in the optimism of new beginnings. I have great friends, a great job, and after a couple of near-death experiences, I deeply appreciate being able to walk around freely under my own steam and swing a hand saw or a cordless drill on occasion. There's really nothing complain about when you look at it that way…

But…*damn!!* I still miss being the Easter Bunny!

The Volcano Diaries

"You can always turn back!"

This was not the most encouraging advice ever given to a hiker thinking about trekking up the side of a dormant volcano where the trail **began** at more than 8,000 feet above sea level and the difficulty rating for the two-and-a-half mile hike in the national park brochure was "strenuous."

Gulp.

But then, I really hadn't been looking for encouragement. I'd been looking for validation...or any other form of an excuse to **not climb the mountain**.

My younger son and I were on a week-long "mom and me" vacation on the West Coast, a trip of particular poignancy because he is the last of the brood, and his departure for college means that my nest will be empty for the first time in twenty-eight years. We had stopped at Lassen Volcanic National Park in northern California at the suggestion of a middle-aged couple we met at Yosemite a couple of days earlier when I volunteered to take their picture.

I had only planned out the first three days of the trip, figuring that we would make it up as we went along, and so we let ourselves get carried to higher altitudes on the descriptive phrases of our newfound acquaintances. This was my most wing-and-a-prayer vacation since I had gone to Ireland when I was twenty-two with a backpack stocked with "instant breakfast" packets, a bicycle that required reassembly once I landed, and phone numbers for some of my Irish cousins.

This time I was (much) older, and (much more) out of shape, and without the resiliency of youth to cushion my missteps. And my left foot had been hurting like heck for the previous four months, making a reusable ice pack and a microwavable heat pack and a bottle of Advil part of my packing essentials.

My son and I had scoped out the park the evening before, after checking into our remote little motel. We picked this place on a recommendation two hundred miles before by the young man who had carved the wooden bear I bought at a gift shop. Are we finding a theme of random adventure here? We were certainly making memories!

One of the most memorable things my son said to me during the entire vacation was, in fact, at that very motel. "Mom," he said, bursting into the room during a phone call to his sweetheart back home, "I think I just heard a cow get attacked by a bear. Do you want to come outside?"

What's a mother to say? Of *course* I stepped outside for a listen. And when the porch lights went out unexpectedly behind us, you wouldn't believe how fast we beat it back into the room!

While he was outside chatting on the phone, I had been poring over the pamphlets and maps we picked up by the park's visitor center. And by the time I went to sleep, I was convinced that between my lifelong acrophobia, the troublesome foot, and the vivid description of altitude sickness that usually sets in *at lower altitudes than we were even going to start hiking at,* I was going to chicken out and insist on a more leisurely walk of half the distance to see a pretty waterfall.

All I was looking for when we pulled up to the park entrance the next morning was an excuse. I pled age, I pled infirmity, I pled forty extra pounds, I pled an appalling lack of stamina...and then I threw in the vertigo and fear of heights for good measure. The heights thing is no laughing matter for me. I get dizzy if I climb higher than the first step on a ladder, and it's been like that for most of my life.

But the cheerful young lady in the Smokey the Bear ranger hat kept trying to steer me in the direction of optimism. Hikers of all ages and sizes were known to have made it to the summit, she said. Drink plenty of fluids to stave off altitude sickness, she advised. And remember, she said, "you can always turn back." I didn't even have to turn my head to know that my son was grinning at the exchange.

185

And so we drove on to the base of the trail that led to Lassen Peak, which topped out at 10,457 feet above sea level. We packed water bottles and granola bars and extra clothes in my son's backpack. There were snow fields even at the trailhead.

I felt out of breath at the first switchback, which was still so close to the parking lot it didn't even list how far we had traveled. I wasn't going for glory here, just endurance, and so I simply kept putting one foot in front of the other, watching my son's heels to keep from feeling dizzy. I had done the exact same thing a few years before as I navigated "Bright Angel Trail" down the side of the Grand Canyon with my daughter. Character building takes many forms.

Near the trailhead, we met a delightful pair of teachers from Florida, Pat and Jackie, who went on hiking adventures during their summers off and had decided to tackle Lassen this time. They each had a good dozen years or more on me, and were taking this adventure in stride. I didn't want to wimp out while they were watching. We often overlapped each other's rest stops along the way. They called out a lot of encouragement to me on the way up.

The higher we climbed, the more breathtaking the views became. The Sierra Nevadas were a distant blue under a nearly cloudless sky. Lake Helen gleamed azure in the park below us. Snow fields were striped pink and white, but the surrounding air was still warm. The forests below looked as tiny as the shrubbery on a model train display. As we scrambled over loose gravel and larger rocks and tree roots, a doe picked her way across the side of the mountain above us, twin fawns scampering quickly behind her to the cover of some brush.

Continuing in the vein of being practical instead of heroic, I took plenty of rest stops along the way, chugging water and letting the faster hikers pass us by. And sometimes even Pat and Jackie! There was usually a tree or two that I could sit under for shade, but inevitably we began to leave the tree line behind. Still, I kept going, watching my son's feet in front of me, occasionally taking his hand to cross the rougher patches.

And then, with less than a mile to the summit, I came to one more switchback and stopped. Up to my left, I could see the trail cross back and forth upon the bare mountain face. And to my right, I could see nothing but open sky.

Right then and there, my fear of heights nailed me to the side of the mountain.

"Robert, honey," I said, "I'm sorry, but I just can't take one more step!" Of all the things that I thought would have shut me down long before—the extra weight, the lack of stamina, the thin air at 9,000 feet, the gimpy foot—it was such an anticlimax to call it quits because of this!

Still, there was no going forward for me, and I sure wasn't going to go back down alone. I folded my fleece sweatshirt into a pad to sit on a nearby rock, took custody of the backpack, and settled in to wait for my son to make it to the summit and bring back some good pictures. It took him a good two hours to get back, which included the half-hour phone call to his girlfriend from the top of the mountain, a lot of picture taking, and some time spent just glorying in the achievement.

As I sat, I basked in the sun and marveled at the grandeur surrounding me, and the total serendipity that had brought us here. Who knew, when we set out on this vacation, that we would be setting out to climb a mountain to its very top? Or photograph a yellow-bellied marmot peeking out of his den near a set of volcanic vents? This was certainly an altitude on the side of a mountain that I never thought I would experience.

A very long time ago, when a friend of mine was getting ready to leave college without graduating and faced a very uncertain future, I sent him on his way with an inspirational poster that read something to the effect that if you set your sights among the heavens, even if you fail you will fall among the stars. I hadn't thought about that in quite a long time, but I thought about it again that day while I sat on the side of the volcano.

At the tail end of our vacation, we drove the well-maintained highway to the visitor center of Mount St. Helens in Washington State. I realized that even though it looked rugged and awesome and high and imposing...we had both made it farther above sea level than this national landmark.

But for me, an even bigger victory was just in getting as far as I had.

I may not have made it to the top of the mountain as I had hoped...but I still ended up sitting high enough that I could nearly touch the stars.

A Hoarder's Revenge

I will be the first to admit that I lead a cluttered—though creative—life.

I grew up surrounded by chaos, both physical and mental, and the apple never fell far from the tree. While I pride myself on the fact that I can **usually** find both my cell phone and my car keys before leaving the house, that's very much the reach of it. The fact weighs on my self-esteem, a diffuse cloud of reprobation invading the edges of my working mind, along with the piles of paper on the grand piano...and the dining room table...and the pool table.

Chaos is my comfort zone, and where there is none, I've been justifiably accused of creating it. Or perhaps it's even more deeply linked to territoriality. I remember the way I would take a stab at housecleaning before the kids came home from college, to greet them with some uncharacteristic tidiness as a sign of affection. The tidiness would get blown to smithereens as soon as the first duffle bags and assorted detritus of travel made it to the top of the stairs and got dumped there. I would look around at the spread of their things, and think, "they're just marking their territory." Thank god they weren't taking after the cat.

After three decades in the same house, with four children who have grown from infancy to adulthood there, I have sentimentally saved a *lot.* Sketches I kept, stretching back to pre-school. School reports. Hand-made Christmas ornaments dating back to the third grade. Ceramic bowls, cups, fruit. Mother's Day cards. And that's just the stuff relating to the kids. I took a look in a deep desk drawer the other day and found canceled checks from an account I had thirty years ago. I think they can finally go in the "burn pile."

I do make the occasional run at making things tidier, more open, more user friendly. The task is endless. It is Herculean. It makes me think of poor Sisyphus of Greek mythology, doomed to repeatedly roll that boulder uphill.

I have no shortage of encouragement on this quest to be a better, neater person. Judy, one of my very BFFs, is wonderfully well organized, as a nurse whose patients' lives depend on her competence should be!! Her frequent prescription is that if I haven't used something in six months, I can safely throw it out. She has come to my rescue on several occasions when I have scheduled big family parties but run out of time to do all the cooking *and* make the place presentable.

Judy whisks into my living room, which I have regarded with a combined state of mental paralysis and horror, and dust, and stack, and artistically place things in different locations. And when she has finished, the room looks "normal" and temporarily inviting,

190

with all seats cleared for sitting. It has sometimes taken me months to locate things that she has reorganized in her zeal, but for the party, it was perfect.

The man in my life does his best as well to nudge me along on the path to neatness, on the theory that my life would be so much easier if I did not have to navigate around piles of junk mail and things that could be recycled. The seventeen years he spent in the Air Force drilled a sense of order and value for spare surroundings into him, and he sets a wonderful example. Periodically, he has come in like a tornado and overhauled a portion of my cluttered life into a remarkably sane example of organization—the garage, for example. My desktop workspace for another. I hold my breath when these projects are done and maintain the order for, say, about two weeks...and then familiar patterns begin to return. He finds it discouraging...but still loves me.

HOWEVER... Once in a while there comes a cosmic flare that puts all that "out after six months" rubbish to shame.

I spent a couple of days looking for my passport for a trip abroad. For some reason it was not in the dresser drawer where it "always" sits. When all was said and done, the passport was out in the car, in the glove compartment, but I didn't know that at the time. But as I ransacked the dresser drawer from front to back, I cast a critical eye on some of the things within it. I decided that along with the gift receipts from purchases made ten years before and the "body shaper" I hadn't fit into for about twenty years, I could also finally throw a historical artifact known as "the flannel bag."

This was a pretty little drawstring bag not even a foot square, in shades of deep turquoise and lavender and black. It had once been the packaging for a matching flannel nightshirt I had bought on impulse while Christmas shopping one year. I actually bought three that day as the Christmas shopping season was drawing to a close—one for myself and two for my daughters. Ten years earlier. I had held on to the bag for that long because it was pretty and because it might "someday" become useful.

Frustrated by my inability to find the passport and infuriated with myself for maintaining such a disorganized home, I recalled Judy's admonitions about the six-month limit, and chucked the bag into the trash under the kitchen sink. I felt a small pang of regret that I had never found a use for such a soft, pretty thing.

Fast forward a couple of days. Weeks earlier, the man in my life had taken it upon himself to bring my dusty binoculars home and clean them thoroughly, freeing them from years of dust and grime and water splashes from the kitchen sink. He brought them back wrapped in a little plastic grocery bag, and I left them there on the table, protected from dust, until I could run to the store and buy something like a quilted tea cozy to protect them on the kitchen counter. That's where I do most my bird watching anyway. For the first many years that I watched birds, as far as I was concerned, if they didn't land on my back porch near the window, they practically didn't exist.

However, I was also getting ready for a road trip, and I wanted to bring the binoculars along in case I found some spare time to bird watch. What could I **possibly** wrap them in so that they wouldn't get dirty and scuffed in the car, but still provid easy access in case a bald eagle briefly flitted into view? The sturdy vinyl carrying case they had originally come with was probably somewhere in my possession...and I knew I would never find it if I searched for a year.

Well, well, well. I'm not too proud to admit that the flannel bag was still sitting at the top of the trash bin in the kitchen. I had gotten a little behind in taking out the trash since banging up a knee and some ribs in a serious fall a few days earlier. And so there, at my fingertips, and even still clean and dry, was the answer to my prayers. In pretty turquoise and black and lavender flannel.

Which, on Judy's "six months and out" timetable, would have decomposed in a landfill about nine years before. And in the world inhabited by the man of my dreams, would have been used as a polishing rag of some sort, possibly involving a car windshield or bumper.

Sigh...!

The bag turned out to be a perfect fit for the binoculars.

And somehow the words "See, I told you so" don't even **begin** to cover the validation I feel!

Tool Time

I had a meltdown last week over a power tool.

The meltdown shouldn't have been surprising. For the past thirty years I've noticed that the first week in October is always the worst for me in terms of emotional troughs and existential despair. I'm sure there's a serious "waning daylight" issue going on. It always passes, with a few days and a lot of chocolate.

What triggered it was a tool that worked just as it was supposed to.

What brought me temporarily to the point of tears, however, was that I knew how to use it. Go figure.

I was in the midst of sanding some storm windows before starting to paint them. There had been a week of splendid painting weather, warm and sunny and dry, and the windows, with their white paint turned a dingy, peeling grey, needed attention before facing the fierce travails of winter.

A shop vac would be involved, of course, to vacuum all the paint chips and dust. I own one. It looks like a sinister cousin of the cloyingly adorable Star Wars droid, R2-D2. But what had brought me to the hardware store and ultimately to the meltdown a few days later was the purchase of both a palm sander and a detail sander.

I bought both of them cheap, as usual. My store brand cordless drill has worked just fine for the past several years and I saw no reason to invest large sums of money in small tools I didn't expect to use much. There was no drama involved in this step, no facing of fears and anxieties of the type that had marked my purchases of first the cordless drill, and then the chain saw.

But somewhere along the line in the days of sanding and painting that followed, my ambivalence toward my newest power tools turned to horror. And when my friend Judy called to say hello one morning, I hit a flashpoint and then dissolved.

Sanding and painting my own storm windows had finally proved the tipping point in a march toward self-sufficiency that seemed, on that bright October morning in a day that would be just a little shorter than the day before, both symbolic and lonely. I finally hung up, dried my tears, blew my nose, and went outside to paint some more.

The man of my dreams, who was tied up busily painting his *own* storm windows and trim during this stretch of idyllic weather, later did his best to point out that firstly, he would love to learn how to use a sewing machine and wouldn't feel his masculinity threatened if he did. And secondly, on a self-sufficiency scale, my chain saw was a *whole* lot more symbolic than a detail sander.

Well, yes. He was right on both counts.

195

But on the other hand, I could milk the subjects of the chain saw and the cordless drill for considerable amount of light cocktail party banter while dressed in stilettos and chiffon and dangling earrings. There was just something about owing a detail sander, however, that bespoke renting space in the "small engines" department of the local hardware store, pulling up a stool at the counter, and debating the finer points of lawn tractor hydraulics. The particular hardware store I'm thinking of is very, very manly. It smells like a combination of oil and metal parts and gas and testosterone. It's a nice place to visit, but I always feel like I've landed briefly on another planet.

I brooded darkly on this new development for a full week.

Then I found myself back in Chicago at the two-flat which had been owned by my godmother and which was about to be sold. I was there to inventory the things that remained, and to help my mother pack up for moving. And so I spent part of the day in my father's work rooms in the basement, poring over the contents, looking to see if there was anything of useful or sentimental value that I wanted to bring home with me.

This place had not been my home. I had lived there for less than a year as a teenager before we picked up stakes and moved to an abandoned farm. I spent another year there after high school, living with my aunt and my grandparents while I worked and took a few classes and contemplated starting college as a full time student. I lived there briefly and yet again for a single summer while in college, working as a legal secretary by day and training my horse at a stable on the edge of the city in the evenings.

It had always been a transitory destination for me.

But my parents had lived there for the past thirty years. And a lot of stuff can build up in a man's work space in that amount of time.

I had not been able to spend much time with my father during those years. Time and distance played a part, family dynamics played another. But I knew all that time that he loved me, and that he was proud of me.

I approached the work rooms with a mix of curiosity and nostalgia and salvage on my mind. There were jars upon jars of used nuts and bolts, screws and nails, drill bits and routers, washers and grinding wheels. Things were stored in coffee cans and boxes, on shelves and on the floor. My mother had been in a wheelchair for most of the past ten years, and so she had not had much to do with things in the basement.

I don't know if the hoarding was a product of my father's mental confusion in his later years, or a by-product of the privations endured as a P.O.W. during and after World War II. But he had worked as a mechanic in the Luftwaffe in Germany during the war, and had worked a succession of factory machine jobs in the U.S. He would have loved the smell and the feel of the "small engines" department in my local hardware store.

Here and there were things I found that I recognized. I rounded up as many drill bits as I could find. I didn't know if they would fit my cordless drill, but I could always figure that out later. Some of drill bits were incredibly tiny, others were enormous. One particular bit was very short, but had a diameter that looked like it was made for cutting woodpecker holes in dead trees. I packed up a couple of hand saws, and a box of wooden kitchen matches.

Sitting on a shelf in shadow was an antique oil can, rusted on the outside but still workable. I tipped it over and pushed on the bottom. A drop of oil squirted on to the workbench. I packed that up to go as well. Cleaned up, the oilcan will sit as a sentimental decoration in my garage. If the Tin Woodsman from the Wizard of Oz ever comes for tea and feels a little stiff, I'll be ready.

High on a shelf in one of the rooms were a couple of Good Housekeeping magazines, more than twenty years old. I pulled them down, wondering what these icons of femininity were doing in such a place. Strangely, they were two copies of the same issue.

When I read through the index, I knew. I had written an essay about the stray dog that chose me for her owner when I was still a teenager up north on the farm, and this was the issue of the magazine it had run in. I looked back at myself from the pages. There were black and white pictures of a much younger version of me cozied up with my husband and two young daughters and the friendly brown-and-white dog with one blue eye. It was my first national by-line, and I smiled. The magazines went into the "take with me" box.

I took a leather "Bell & Howell" camera bag, stiff with age. I have my father's old camera somewhere in my home. A Craftsman folding metal ruler, and a pair of wire cutters made the grade as well. A side benefit of spending time with the man of my dreams has been that I've learned that Craftsman tools are something special, not only because of quality but because they come with a lifetime guarantee.

And then I found the capstone to this journey through time—my father's Craftsman electric drill. It was heavy, with a steel casing and thick rubber cord, and a tiny drill bit still fixed in position. It looked nothing like a drill does today. It had something of that retro "futuristic" look of the giant robot in the original black-and-white version of "The Day the Earth Stood Still" with Michael Rennie and Patricia Neal.

Lifetime guarantee?

"Ha!" I thought. If this thing ever needed parts, customer service would be contacting a museum.

Pressed for time, I did not test the drill, but simply took it along instead and went upstairs to pack some china. Whether the drill worked or not, I didn't care. I felt somehow closer to the man who had tried again and again to teach me how to change a tire when I was sixteen. I never committed the instructions to memory. Now I can just call the American Automobile Association on my cell phone.

When I returned home, I plugged the drill into an electric socket in the garage and pulled the trigger. It roared to life with a scream much larger than its size implied. I smiled and coiled up the cord, and placed it carefully on a shelf in my new workbench in the garage, next to the palm sander.

I will be my father's daughter. I will step up proudly to my detail sander. And I will quit pouting over the fact that I know what a socket wrench is.

Because when I left Chicago that day I brought home the wrench...and all the sockets I could find as well.

Ghosts in the Pasture

The weeds in the empty, unused paddock grew five feet high and more, and I parted them gingerly with my hands as I walked across sandy soil to the pasture fence.

No horses lived there anymore. There had been no equine hooves churning the ground impatiently this summer, prancing and pounding it to bare dirt as I approached for the morning turn-out. Nature abhors a vacuum, and a phantasmagorical forest of lacy and slender foliage sprang gracefully from the windswept soil, a tall, swaying barricade to be traversed before yielding the keys to memory.

I had not begun with this goal in mind. All I set out to accomplish that morning was three quick turns around the edge of my property at a brisk walk for some desperately needed exercise. Drenching rains and pressure cooker temperatures had combined recently to hatch a vicious crop of mosquitoes, and venturing outside had become like armed warfare. The bugs were winning, the humans cowering behind screens and air conditioners and aerosol cans of smelly insect repellant.

But the weather had turned unseasonably cold, and the chilly morning air and a stiff wind had temporarily parted the veil of bloodsucking pests. It was time to press the advantage, and make the most of a walk in the woods before it turned warm and tropic again.

I walked happily up and down the hills and across the fields, down a path overhung in places with evergreen branches and through a meadow shot through with morning glories and milkweed. My route took me alongside the pasture where the horses had grazed every summer for two decades. Brush had grown up along the fence line over the past few years, making the posts and woven wire nearly invisible.

I reveled in the sunlight as I walked, and the wind felt clean and cool on my face. Not much occupied my mind but the sights and smells around me. A handful of wild mushrooms here, a discarded turkey feather there, pine cones and dead branches, a sumac leaf prematurely turning blood red in a field of green, heralding the inevitable end of summer. I occasionally thought of what new perennials I'd like to buy next for the flower beds.

But I slowed as I reached the wooden paddock fence at the end of my last lap, and stopped to look in. The paddock was empty. The last of the horses had died the winter before. The steel water tanks lay tipped forlornly on their sides where they had rested for nearly a year, and the place felt strangely silent. There were no snorts of recognition, no sound of hoofbeats thudding, no hearty knocks and scraping noises as feed buckets clattered on their hooks while the two horses dove in to their twice-daily race to the bottom. It was always a competition, where the fastest eater then tried to get seconds by shouldering aside the slower one.

I had never seen it like this, and I unlatched the gate. Tall grass had sprung up undisturbed around the base, and it took some tugging to dislodge. The wood had weathered to a splintered, silvery grey from years of sun and rain and snow.

I left the gate standing open. There was no need to bolt it behind me anymore. The casualness went against the grain of thirty-odd years of habit in owning horses and cutting off their escape. I passed the two-sided shed in the corner of the paddock where they had weathered countless rain and snow storms, and took cover from the blazing sun on the summers' hottest days. It felt like a ghost town.

The new forest of weeds finally stood behind me, and I struggled a bit with the heavy gate to the pasture itself. It stood in a break between lines of tall evergreens. I stepped through, into the sunlight and three acres of pasture. The grass, ungrazed and untrampled, was deeper and more lush than I had ever seen it. The purple clover had long since stopped flowering, but a field of Queen Anne's lace spread across the middle. There was still a bare groove in the dirt approaching the paddock, worn by two decades of the horses answering the call to the evening feeding at a trot or even a gallop. New saplings sprang up at random, with no one left to chew them down.

I walked entirely to the far side of the pasture, something I had rarely done when Hoki and Babe were still alive. Then, my priority was usually to call them in for a feeding or a rendezvous with the veterinarian or the farrier. Vaccinations, hoof trims, examinations for various ailments...there was always an air of urgency and impatience to calling them back to closed quarters.

This time, I had the twin luxuries of time and reverie. A flock of two dozen cedar waxwings flitted from branch to branch in a dead tree as I passed underneath. I looked for the flock of wild turkeys that had often frequented the pasture, but didn't see or hear them then.

Memories came back as I walked, picturesque snapshots from the past. The hard times were forgotten, nailed shut and buried. There were no thoughts of blizzards, rain storms, colic, middle-of-the-night trips to freezing barns, heartbreaks and desperate measures. The only images that surfaced this day were short, and fragmented, and beautiful.

Babe, the palomino, looking like an equine pin-up in a field of flowers, ears pitched forward and brown eyes wide and alert. Hoki, the buckskin, trotting gamely along on arthritic legs to answer the dinner bell, his gait the sign of an old man, but his dappled coat gold and beautiful and, until his last year, still youthful. Babe, wheeling and prancing playfully, or rolling freely in the dirt to scratch her back. Hoki, mentally quite feeble but still utterly devoted to his female companion, master of his one-horse "herd." I finally turned back, feeling very lucky.

As I reached the paddock again, I stopped to check out the emergency fence repairs I had made a couple of years before. I still have the cordless drill I bought that same day, and the confidence I gained from having to use it. The boards I sawed and drilled and fastened still looked new. But the twine scaffolding I left hanging from one had disappeared, no doubt turned into nesting material by some bird or mouse in the neighborhood. The pasture gate swung shut more easily this time, and I fastened it one last time out of habit. It would keep no one in or out anymore.

Then I made my way across the sand and back through the ghostly weeds. I tugged the second gate firmly into place, shot the bolt home...and closed the gate on the past.

The Sisterhood of the Chop Saw

My son looked at me and my accoutrements with skepticism through narrowed eyes. This would be the son with the tattoo between his shoulder blades, the hand-rolled cigarette, the assortment of earrings, and the riot of curls that—at the right length—give him a jaunty, ***Viva la Revolución*** Che Guevara vibe.

He's a hard one to impress when it comes to wardrobe unorthodoxy. But impress—or stun—I did.

"Mom, you look like you're ready to break into a chemical plant." From out of the mouths of babes.

I would be lying if I said I took this assessment calmly. Rather, I had caught a reflection of myself in a window just a few seconds before, and was already hovering on the edge of hysterical laughter.

It was ninety degrees out, and I was decked out in a tank top, with a wet bandana across the lower two-thirds of my face like a bank robber in the Old West. I sported safety goggles over my tri-focals; giant padded vinyl ear protectors that would have blocked the decibels on an airport runway; and a pair of green suede work gloves. I personally thought I looked like a galactic bounty hunter straight out of "Star Wars."

My son started to laugh, and that's all I needed to become completely unglued. When the safety goggles finally started to steam up as I doubled over, I was done for. I pulled off the scarf, the ear mufflers, the gloves and the goggles, and laughed and laughed, holding on to the porch railing to stay upright, until tears came to my eyes.

I kept laughing until I got just about all of it out, then suited up again. One piece at a time, I covered up for the job. Scarf. Goggles. Ear protectors. Work gloves.

Because all kidding aside, operating a chop saw is not a laughing matter!

My composure marginally reclaimed, I finally approached the reason for all that caution—a rented "chop saw" sitting on the tailgate of a Ford F-150 pickup truck. It certainly looked like nothing I would ever find in my kitchen.

The saw had a circular blade about a foot in diameter. The blade pivoted up and down, ready to slice through concrete, metal, wood, and errant limbs with lethal efficiency. It looked dangerous just sitting there, lurking beneath its bright red metal safety guard. It was about to give a whole new dimension to my acquaintance with power tools.

Wow, how things change.

Six months earlier, I had never heard the words "chop" and "saw" used in the same sentence. I was feeling mighty pleased with myself, in fact, about acquiring a cordless drill and a battery-operated chain saw after the divorce and not being afraid to use them. Really, I thought, I was pretty well set with a couple of hammers, a set of hex wrenches, some screwdrivers and a retractable tape measure.

Then my aunt passed away, and I spent hours driving back and forth to Chicago with my friend Mary Kay to organize the estate sale. As the miles sped by, the topic of putting in a brick patio next to the house came up, and I picked my friend's brain for suggestions.

Mary Kay is a very handy gal, able to pull off both spike heels with a slinky black evening dress and home improvement projects with aplomb and panache. She is far more experienced than I when it comes to wielding a hammer, and routinely takes a more active role in shaping her environment. I tend to get backed into making repairs because things break, such as pasture fences, or when dead trees fall down where they shouldn't. The most initiative and daring I show usually involves a paint roller.

Mary Kay, on the other hand, has been known to dismantle and reconstruct her foyer while her husband was away on business for a few days, just for the fun of it. When it comes to using power tools, she not only talks the talk, she walks the walk. I was learning at the feet of the master.

"You're going to need a chop saw," she said as I drove, and I duly made a mental note. I had no idea what a chop saw was, but I was assured that one was needed for cutting bricks. And as a person with her heart set on a herringbone brick pattern, I understood that some bricks indeed would require cleaving.

Months later, with both the estate sale and the winter snow cover behind us, the plan was finally ready to roll. There were pallets of concrete paving bricks and sand stacked in the driveway, lumber ready to be picked up for framing, two brand new shovels, and a weather forecast that was warm and dry. Most importantly, I also had a supply of "volunteer" labor in the form of three of my children, one of their friends, and the man in my life.

Don't think that *that* didn't take some coordinating! I had cagily played the "let's celebrate Mother's Day late!" card. It worked.

I had spent the day before the patio project cooking nearly non-stop to feed this busy crew. I naively assumed that once I had picked up the saw from the equipment rental place, my job duties would consist mainly of finishing the potato salad, keeping the beer cold, and bringing food out from time to time.

The best laid plans...

By the time we actually started, it was one in the afternoon. Since the man in my life was the only one among us who had any experience at all with laying bricks or in building and setting a wooden frame, the job of cutting the concrete pavers suddenly shifted to me. Wielding a pencil and a calculator while sitting in the shade, I figured out that setting this particular pattern would require cutting a minimum of eighteen pavers into two parts. Never let it be said that you won't use basic math after high school!

We measured the first brick and lined up the metal guide together, and then he pushed the "on" switch and set the blade whirling. As blade met concrete, the noise level ramped from loud to absolutely searing. A huge cloud of dust erupted and hung in the air, drifting toward the garage and filling the truck with fine white powder. He stood back, incredulous at the magnitude of the mess a single brick had left behind. Erring on the side of caution, I knew there were nineteen more to go.

Well, he said with a shrug, the beauty of having an old truck is that you can mess it up and there's no harm done. Cleanup would come later, when he could park it facing uphill and run a hose over the inside. We left the chop saw on the back of the truck, and I gamely stepped in for the rest of the job. After I quit laughing.

Thank God for ear protectors. And safety goggles. And a wet cotton bandana to repeatedly soak and cover my face with! Even with my ears covered, I could feel the screaming noise through the vibration of the machine. I felt a primitive, visceral sense of pride at watching the cloud of dust kick up as the blade cut a slot through one side of the brick. Then, a short pause while I turned the brick over, lined it up again, and steadily cut through the rest.

The newly cut side was a thing of wondrous, smooth beauty, especially when compared to the alternative method of hitting it with a hammer and chisel. Running the saw was absolutely empowering and frightening all in one. And my triceps ached for two days afterward just from the effort of pushing the blade downward into concrete again and again.

Driving to work the next day, after I had returned the saw to the rental shop, I called Mary Kay to bring her up to speed on my patio adventures. When I got to the part describing my outlandish outfit and my son's remarks, both of us were sputtering and laughing so hard we could barely talk.

"Feels pretty good, doesn't it?" she asked.

Yup, I admitted, it sure did.

A little later as I drove, I thought about a much younger attorney I had worked with, and found myself grinning from ear to ear. A few years earlier I had come to work one day and stopped by his office next to mine, regaling him with my weekend exploits of buying my first hand saw to cut branches that had fallen across a hiking path. At least I *think* it was the story about the hand saw. It might have been the cordless drill adventure.

"That settles it, Mary," he said. "You are officially manlier than I am!"

Well then, I thought. If he had so been impressed with my hand saw, what would he think about cutting concrete pavers off the back of a pickup truck?

I didn't have to wait long to find out. When I got to work I found an email message from this very man waiting for me, asking about the status of a case I had argued before the state supreme court months ago. We traded thoughts about the case, and then I filled him in on the "chop saw" afternoon.

He was impressed, but he also stressed that now that he was married and a homeowner to boot, he felt like he was finally starting to catch up to me. He had just finished remodeling a bathroom, in fact, and was now well acquainted with the art of cutting tiles. We were both justifiably proud of the ground we had covered, me since my divorce, him since he was a young single guy living in an apartment.

I suppose, if he really makes nice, Mary Kay and I will officially admit him into the Sisterhood of the Chop Saw.

And if he sends us both imported chocolate, we may even waive the part about the spike heels.

Love in the Time of Cupcakes

The last of the "tennis ball" cupcakes set sail this morning, a small but telling harbinger of the fact that I'm going to be facing an empty nest in the fall. Twenty-seven years of "hands on" mothering, symbolically reduced to two dozen clumps of devil's food cake in little foil baskets. They swooshed out the door with my youngest son, for what would be his last tennis meet of high school. He graduates in another couple of weeks, heading for college in the fall, and instantly turning any reference to the words "high school" into the past tense.

I have been making cupcakes decorated like tennis balls—light yellow frosting with the slightest tinge of green, arced with curves and swoops of white icing—for fourteen years now, ever since my oldest daughter signed up for freshman girls' tennis before the school year even started. Call me OCD, I don't mind. I consider it a badge of honor.

There are fundamental differences between "girls' tennis" and "boys' tennis" and only some of them have to do with testosterone levels. Girls' tennis season starts in late summer and continues barely to the leading edge of fall, guaranteeing splendid and warm afternoons and entire weekend days watching limber young ladies flit around on the court in bouncing pony tails and flippy little matching skirts, their suntanned legs flying. Girls' tennis, from my experience on the sidelines, involves matching hair doo-dads with color coordinated ribbons, team posters, lots of conversation, and a great appreciation for cute snacks. Hence the tennis ball cupcakes, a big hit with my daughters and their teams for many years.

Boys' tennis, on the other hand, starts on the cusp of very early spring, when winter hangs on for dear life. Here in the upper Midwest, winter's claws are deep. More than one tennis season for my sons has started its first practice as snowflakes were falling. The weather leans more toward rain, and cold, and wind, and if there is coffee involved for blanket-wrapped spectators under grey, stormy skies, the coffee has been hot, not iced. Very few boys sported pony tails, and nobody wore matching barrettes. The guys still appreciated the cupcakes...but I don't think that they even noticed the decorative frosting right before they inhaled them.

And still, despite the fact that for years my cupcakes have been hastily vaporized (without a single squeal of how "cute" they were) by my sons and their teammates, I clung to tradition. At least once a season I needed to send those sweet, fluffy treats along to a meet, even if—as the years went by and my job schedule got less flexible—another mother would actually have to deliver them for me. Call me crazy, it's been done before.

While the "tennis ball cupcakes" stretch back fourteen years, the cupcake thing has actually a fixture for a decade more. Back to when my oldest daughter needed to bring a birthday treat for kindergarten. Or preschool.

So through the next twenty-odd years, these miniature confections were a constant and a comfort amid the multi-tasking, crisis-response mentality that goes into raising four kids with a minimum number of emergency room visits. There were cupcakes with sprinkles for birthdays, cupcakes with candy dots for art shows, cupcakes decorated like little ghosts and jack-o-lanterns for Halloween.

This last tradition—the Halloween cupcakes—nearly drove me into the ground one year.

I had three children in the same grade school at the same time. The youngest wanted Halloween cupcakes for his second grade class party. I signed on for two dozen, half of them frosted orange and half of them white, with little ghost outlines and pumpkin smiles drawn on with melted chocolate, and eyes made from chocolate chips. Then the fifth grader chimed in. I signed on to bake another two dozen.

And then as I started baking, I thought of my daughter's eighth grade class going without my special treats on this festive day, and I threw caution to the wind. Halfway through decorating seventy-two little ghosts and jack-o-lanterns with liquid chocolate, I rethought my rash enthusiasm...but it was too late to turn back.

I was planning to dress up in costume for the second graders' party, and I teased my daughter with the thought of showing up in said costume to deliver the goods. She's got a dark, sultry beauty to her, and she warned me off.

"Mom, don't you dare!!" she said ominously, her eyes flashing like the fiery gypsy in "Carmen." I filed that thought in the "hmmm...maybe" pile. I made some soothing mention about bringing along a change of clothes.

The next day I precariously loaded six dozen cupcakes into the minivan, and set off for school. The fifth grade cupcakes were dropped off and put out of mind. The second grade Halloween party was so cute it could make your back teeth hurt. The class put on a teeny tiny little play, and my son wore a pint-sized royal blue cape I had sewn with a fake ermine collar for his role as the king.

And then the lunch bell rang. I grabbed the last two dozen cupcakes from the van and walked them down the length of the school to my daughter's eighth grade classroom. Her back was to me as I stood in the doorway. The friend she was chatting with looked up, and announced slyly, "Sarah, your mom is here."

Slowly she turned...and there I stood, the cardboard box full of treats utterly overshadowed by my appearance in a Pocahontas-style beige fringed tunic with red embroidered trim, black leggings, and a feather in my hair. I bit back a grin, but it was *really* hard.

My daughter flashed daggers at me with those dark brown eyes. If looks could have killed, I'd be long dead. But at the same time, despite her fourteen-year-old peer-fueled fury and

216

embarrassment, I could see the corners of her mouth begin to curl up in a smile in spite of herself, at the sheer *perversity* of my guest appearance. I delivered the goods and quickly exited stage left, fighting back a laugh.

Eight years later she and I chatted on the phone as I drove to drop off yet another batch of tennis ball cupcakes for her younger brother's meet the next day. I was going to have to miss this contest too, and so once again the cupcakes were going to stand in for me, making me feel like I was still sharing a part of the adventure. We shared a good laugh about the day I showed up dressed like Pocahontas at her eighth grade classroom. At the age of twenty-two, you develop a lot more perspective and forgiveness for antics like that.

I bemoaned the fact that now that she was in college, I no longer had the opportunity to bring festive or seasonal or downright ridiculous treat to her classes anymore.

"Mom, you can bring cupcakes to my class any time!" she assured me. "We'll eat 'em!"

I could not resist pushing the envelope. If it was around Halloween, I asked, could I wear the Pocahontas costume again? There was just an instant of hesitation, then she said "okay!"

I could just imagine her eyes rolling across the miles between us. Maturity comes in many forms, and learning to humor a mother during a fleeting moment of insanity is a remarkable milestone for a daughter of any age.

I never did drive the eighty miles to one of her college classrooms after that to bring a sugary treat to a bunch of accomplished and sophisticated college students. Life just got a little too busy, though in hindsight I wish I'd grabbed the opportunity.

But I still remember laughing at the memory with her, and the beautiful thread of give-and-take the offer and its acceptance held, binding us tightly and preciously with love and affection despite the distance.

They were just cupcakes.

And then some.

Angels in the Snow

I can still remember the snow falling in buckets and clumps. It fell relentlessly, drenching the landscape, cloaking the interstate, and obscuring any sense of where one lane ended and another began, muffling the brightness of the far-off street lights like a scrim on a theater stage.

My daughter and I could see the street lights above empty, wind-swept streets below as we passed by the highway exit that had been our best hope of finding a motel and waiting out the storm. The exit sign had finally emerged in the blizzard, but too quickly for us to safely change lanes on the slippery, snow-covered highway. And so we kept on, white-knuckling it through the storm.

Surely, we thought, we would get off at the very next exit, wherever that would be. We weren't in the middle of the Gobi desert or Antarctica. This was the American Midwest. There had to be a motel somewhere nearby, a modern place with central heating and clean sheets and a bathroom. A place where we would admit that a blizzard in northern Wisconsin had proven that there existed some times when you should just stay home and wait it out. I cautiously and slowly edged the minivan into the right lane—or what seemed to be a lane—and kept watching the dark side of the highway for a another snow-covered green blur that would be our salvation.

My daughter pored over a map of Wisconsin by a tiny reading light above the dashboard. If that last exit was Menomonee, there had to be smaller towns up ahead.

We had started the journey hours earlier, a familiar three-hundred-mile trek from our home in southern Wisconsin to the Twin Cities where my daughter was a college student. Sometimes her dad drove her and I stayed home to hold down the fort, and sometimes I drove. The trip one-way took a good six hours in good weather.

The weather had indeed been good when we started, that much was true. There were a few snowflakes falling as we pulled out of the driveway, but four-wheel-drive can make you cocky. The weather forecasters were predicting snow in our path, but who ever expected total accuracy from the weatherman? We blithely set out in daylight, with the goal of making it to the Twin Cities not far off our usual pace.

As daylight faded, the snow picked up. For about an hour we vacillated over whether it was getting heavy enough to justify benching ourselves at a motel until morning, or whether it was starting to lighten up. Wishful thinking can be so disarming. And with every mile we drew closer to our destination, with the tantalizing thought of completing our journey without interruption.

220

As we sailed past the exit and watched the street lights sink into a swirling void behind us, we finally knew we had overreached. Still, we were confident that a room for hire would soon be ours and we would be safely out of the storm. I drove cautiously, slowly, along the set of tire tracks cut in the snow by the drivers ahead. There appeared to be only one lane left to use, and every car on the road that night seemed to follow an unwritten rule to stay in that single lane, guided by the faint pinprick of taillights in the distance assuring that there was still a road to find, like hikers traversing a narrow ledge single file.

And then that fragile arrangement fell apart.

There are instants in your life when you don't know if you will live or die, and we suddenly faced ours.

From out of the swirling, snowy blackness, a set of headlights perched higher than ours came up on our left. A semi-trailer whose driver clearly had less patience than anyone else on the road inexorably crept up on us, bearing down closer and closer. I could see the truck's headlights casting their beams of light through the driving snow, and I focused totally on keeping the minivan straight and completely in its lane.

The truck never touched us. But as it passed, the wind force it created caught the minivan like a giant hand and sent us sliding off at an angle, completely out of control. I remember noting that the sides of the truck were yellow and white as our headlights turned toward the giant machine as it passed us methodically, implacably, like Leviathan cleaving the silent, wine-dark sea.

221

As the truck drew away from us and disappeared into the dark, a drift of snow swirled off its roof and plunged us into total whiteout. We slewed and yawed blindly out of control. I turned the wheel desperately back and forth, trying to get some purchase beneath the wheels, but my efforts were useless.

After a couple of seconds that seemed like a lifetime, we felt the front of the minivan hit something hard. A guardrail had kept us from sliding into a ditch or worse.

"Honey, are you okay?" I asked.

"Sure," my daughter replied. "How about you?"

I was fine too…but as I looked toward her, I could also see pinpoints of light that signaled the approach of the next car in the single snow-covered lane. We realized instantly that our minivan, positioned crosswise across the lane of traffic, would be invisible in the storm to oncoming cars until it would be too late to stop. I slammed the van into reverse and hoped that luck would go our way. If it didn't, we would have to get out of the van and over the guardrail before the next accident happened.

The wheels caught, and we pushed back into the lane of traffic. Slowly we drove on, and found the next exit only a mile or two later. The road it led to had barely been plowed. The map showed a small town a few miles north, and we aimed the damaged van that way with hope in our hearts. We were deep in the middle of nowhere. The few driveways that we passed were unplowed and dark and uninviting. No sign announcing a town ahead was anywhere to be seen.

We finally drew near what seemed to be a farm, with a tall yard light silhouetted in the falling snow, and a large sign out front that gave it an air of respectability. The driveway looked as if it had been plowed at some point during the storm. We drove up to a small house. I left my daughter in the car, and knocked on the door.

A young woman answered, her eyes cautious and wary. We had been in an accident on the interstate, I explained, and were trying to find a place to stay. The map said that we'd find a town in this direction. Were we on the right track?

No, she answered. The town ahead no longer had any type of lodging. More important, she warned us, there was a dangerous and winding hill not far ahead of us on this road, and we should *not* try to navigate it in this storm.

Well then, I replied. My daughter and I clearly needed a place to stay in this storm. We were easy keepers. Could we just pay her forty dollars to sleep on her kitchen floor?

The young woman said she was sorry, but that she would have to refuse. She had her young children in the house, and her husband was away from home, and she simply did not feel comfortable with letting two strangers into the house while he was away. We would just have to get back on the interstate and keep driving.

I returned to the car, crushed and absolutely stunned. Ahead of us lay a road we had no business being on. Behind us lay the interstate where we had nearly died. The seaworthiness of the van

223

was a wild card. My daughter busied herself with brushing and scraping the snow from the windows as I tried to inventory the damage to the front end and determine whether or not the van would be able to make it much farther. I called my husband to report on the night's events and tell him that we were safe so far…but uncertain as to where we would end up.

A man with a beard and a dark snow-covered jumpsuit came up to my side of the van out of nowhere as I shut down the phone and tried to figure out what to do next. I was startled, but rolled down the window and explained our situation. He thought for a minute, then had us follow him to a trailer located behind the home where we had just been turned away. He explained that his wife was out for a little while, and so he couldn't commit just then to letting us stay the night. But at least we could get out of the cold.

We followed obediently and gratefully…and when the pair of them were finally together, they must have decided we posed no hazard, and folded us into their tiny, cramped home. As the snow continued to mount outside and we finally tucked into some warm food, we exchanged our stories.

The young woman who had turned us away was in fact their daughter-in-law, they said. Until recently, the man with the beard and his wife had lived in a state much farther east. But their only son was a farmer here in Wisconsin. And when it appeared that he needed help to keep the farm running, they had willingly left their comfortable life behind and moved here to help him keep his business and his family on solid ground. It was not the life they had predicted, but it was the one they chose without hesitation.

My daughter and I slept in their bed that night, utterly exhausted but warm and safe. By morning, the storm had passed and the skies had cleared and the sunlight positively glistened on the newly fallen carpet of snow. We scraped the heavy blanket of white off the van and said our goodbyes and heartfelt thanks. I slipped a fifty-dollar bill on to a nearby shelf before we left. I knew that they would refuse it if I mentioned it to them before we drove off.

My daughter and I retraced our path eight miles back to the exit we wished we had taken the night before, and dropped off the van at an auto repair shop to get checked before continuing on. The whole world seemed swept clean, a glorious radiance and purity to the snow cover that extended to the horizon. The highway surface itself, plowed clean in the middle of the night, looked as well-maintained as if Martha Stewart had been running the road crew. We chowed down over pancakes and sausage and pondered the strangeness of fortune and the kindness of strangers.

Many years have now passed since that desperate night in the snow. A snow-covered road still frightens me far more than it used to. When I look back, I know that I have never been closer to being dead than at that instant when our car spun out of control in blinding snow in the wake of an enormous, anonymous truck. I wonder often at the workings of fate, and the hand of God, and the presence of angels. There is a lot that I'll never know.

But I know for sure that every so often angels appear in our lives when we need them most. The come without wings or halos, celestial choirs or golden flutes or harps.

And once in a while, they may just show up dressed for the occasion, wearing a watch cap and sturdy Sorel boots and a dark blue snowmobile suit.

Full Circle

If living well, as they say, is the best revenge, I was sure having a red-letter day in the payback department.

Starting from the top down, I was standing in front of a buffet table of canapés that were both expensive and absolutely delicious. The holiday gathering was double-billed as a wine tasting event, so while my left hand held a beaded little black evening purse, the right held a long-stemmed glass filled with a German Eiswein. I love sweet German wines, and so this was right up my alley for taste.

I was decked out in iridescent chandelier earrings and a sparkly white see-through sweater, with a Victoria's Secret satin camisole keeping me both decent and legal. A plum-colored cut velvet skirt and black suede sling-back Brazilian high heels with tiny bows rounded out the ensemble.

I had bought the shoes on impulse the winter before, spending more than I ever do—and paying full price, which I almost **never** do!—in a defiant act of faith that at some point, I was going to have someplace to wear them to. I'm a big believer that if you buy the shoes, the occasion will follow.

I was newly divorced and happy about it, and my ex—who would normally be at this yearly affair since by all rights it was *his* bar association's Christmas party—was spending the evening home with our younger children. And as I stood by the buffet table, savoring the good food and the great company, an attorney who originally knew me as just "the spouse" at these gathering for nearly two decades, came up, his wife beside him, and asked "So…what can you tell me about the judges in your county?"

I cheerfully and obligingly held court. I had been in my job as a state prosecutor in another county for a good five years, so I gave him a complete, humorous rundown. I eventually wound down the evening swapping courtroom tales of valor with a group of young attorneys who had graduated from law school about the same time I did just a few years earlier. For the first time since I had been going to these festivities, I felt like I had my own posse—if just for an evening—and it felt really, really good.

It had not been the most auspicious of evenings to start with. I had only agreed to attend the day before, in part because the organizers were still trying to fill the tables. Guilt over never paying my dues to the group—except for the year I graduated from law school so that I could claim my place in the big group photo—tended to keep me at home for most of these things. And there was a blizzard in progress too.

On the other hand, the party was only a couple of miles from my house. I was still driving my Subaru, which was like sitting in a four-wheel-drive tank. And after the divorce, it seemed symbolically important to show up at some of the same things I had attended as part of a married couple for years, just to fly the flag and show that I was still standing. Whether this would cut down on local gossip or throw fuel on the fire, I did not know. But that wasn't the point. I just needed to show my face. And smile.

It really turned out to be a great evening. It wasn't until the next day, however, that the hand of irony struck me full force. Because I had been in the exact same knot of conversation seventeen years earlier, with the exact same people. The same attorney, and his wife, and myself. The only person missing from the tableau was my ex-husband. And the contrast couldn't have been deeper, or more moving, or more revealing in terms of a life journey.

Seventeen years before, I had been seven months pregnant with my third child. This was our first big local bar association outing, a semi-annual gathering of most of the local lawyers, their spouses, and a guest speaker or some type of entertainment. My husband had recently taken a job with a local firm. I was as big as a house, and clad in a cheap, tent-sized floral maternity dress. We were all dressed up for dinner, and the entire thing—and all the people in it—were brand new to me. I really, really hoped that I would make a good impression. And that people would like me.

And in that setting, I was entirely peripheral. As the stay-at-home wife and mother, I was nearly invisible. I gravitated naturally to the other wives, and we swapped tales of motherhood and girl scouting and cake baking and carpooling. I might have mentioned that I was a free-lance writer, but I don't remember. The scene would be repeated for many years.

Most of the attorneys (at least in the beginning) were men, and they gathered in groups like pin-striped gladiators, swapping tales of courtroom adventures and victories won and appeals mounted and opponents thwarted and justice demanded. The whole arena had a heavy testosterone base under the wall-to-wall carpeting of the country club dining room.

As the years rolled by, there were channel markers and growth rings and metaphorical roots to trip over along the way. The riding accident that put me in the body cast. Law school. The discovery that my brain not only still worked, it worked better than it had when I went to college the first time. My youngest child starting kindergarten, and my oldest leaving for college.

There were a few memorable meltdowns, a couple of them in the exquisite Gothic church where I had been married. Arguing a case, and then another, and then another before the state supreme court. And finally—a long time in coming—the divorce. One step up, two steps back, a couple forward again, a side step here and there.

And so the contrast between those two face-to-face encounters with the same attorney, seventeen long and arduous years apart, stood out in my mind as a token of validation, with the brightness of a diamond in a platinum setting on a sunny day. Just look how far I'd come!! The irony made me feel warm and tingly all over. Like a snapshot of victoriously reaching that peak you attempted to climb on vacation, in utter defiance of your better judgment and common sense and aching muscles.

That was then. One thing you can always count on in life is that if you're actually living it instead of just watching from the sidelines, there will always be more channel markers and more stumbling blocks and more growth rings along the way.

Since that delightful evening when I stood sipping German wine while decked out in velvet and Victoria's Secret, I've gone through a lot more. The "year of turbo dating." The loss of both my father and godmother after terrible health complications. The serious illnesses of two of my children. Hundreds of miles on the back of a Harley, and my *youngest* child leaving for college. And two more command performances before the state supreme court.

Just like that vacation snapshot of conquering the summit, the picture fades in importance as the life being lived just gets bigger. Gloriously, messily, sometimes tragically, oftentimes joyfully… bigger. And so inevitably, I revisit the snapshot less and less often. There will always be more hills ahead.

But it doesn't mean that I've forgotten the climb to get this far.

I've still got the Brazilian spike heels to prove it.

About the Author

"It's never too late to make mid-course corrections!"

Mary T. Wagner is a former newspaper and magazine journalist who changed careers at forty, going to law school and becoming a criminal prosecutor. However, she never **could** step away from the written word entirely, and inevitably the joy of writing drew her back to the keyboard.

Her slice-of-life essays have often been described as both "inspiring" and "empowering," and have won numerous national and regional awards.

Wagner's life experiences includes the defining watershed of motherhood, and stints as a girl scout troop leader, truck stop waitress, office temp, judicial clerk, and radio talk show host. She counts both wearing spike heels and learning to use a cordless drill and chain saw among her "late blooming" discoveries, and would be hard pressed to surrender either her favorite stilettos or her power tools.

DISCUSSION GUIDE

1. In the essay "Of Shoes and Strategy," Mary describes her "turning point" in footwear, going from sneakers and sensible shoes to spike heels for the first time when midway through her forties. What do you think that first pair of stiletto heels *really* symbolized in her life?

2. Mary describes wrenching transitions in her life when she was a teenager in "Cookie Therapy." How do you think her past family relationships affect her relationships with her children? Do chocolate chip cookies really make everything better?

3. In the essay "Turbo Dating—A Year in Review," Mary describes jumping into the dating world with both feet after 25 years of marriage. What did you think of her kamikaze approach? In retrospect, do you think she should have waited longer before making that transition? Was she brave, dumb, headstrong, or some other combination?

4. In "Ripple Effect," Mary shares the story of how her life and career path was changed by someone else's encouragement, and reminds her children that "kindness is never wasted." Has there been a time in your life when someone's belief in you has pushed you farther than you thought you could go?

5. In "Love in Wood and Wax," Mary talks about how her definitions and understanding of "romance" and "romantic gestures" have changed over time. Have yours? Is that a good thing or not? If they have, do you still miss the old patterns?

6. After her divorce, Mary's transition in tools went by necessity from cupcake pans and a hand-mixer to the chain saw and a tool kit. Can you see yourself in her shoes? Are you in them already? What was the last tool you used and what for?

7. In "Return to the Fatherland," Mary writes of taking her elderly father and her teenaged sons to Germany for a reunion with their relatives, only to find en route that his mind was far more fragile than she had known. The roles of parent and child immediately and sadly changed. Did the trip have the result that she had wanted? What good things came from the journey despite her father's increasing frailty? Do you think that her sons learned more from it than they expected to as well?

8. In "The Island," Mary describes renting a cabin in a vacation spot she had only experienced before this with her husband and children, long before the divorce. Her stated intention was to spend the week writing in peace and quiet. Was that the most important thing she took away from it? Could it have gone badly instead? How would YOU step out of your "pressure cooker" life for a week?

9. Mary has often been described as "living in the moment," letting serendipity guide her choices and experiences. Do you enjoy that as well in your own life...or does that "make it up as you go" quality drive you bonkers? Why or why not? Would you trust her to pack your suitcase before a trip abroad?

10. In "The Volcano Diaries," Mary abandons her quest to reach the summit of a mountain because of her fear of heights...but eventually realizes that she has still gone farther than she thought she could. Is there a time you have "fallen short" in your own life's journey that still feels like a success of sorts? Do you think that people learn more from success or failure?

11. Do you think that Mary's introduction to gardening also made her grow as a person? What does her flower garden symbolize for her? Have you had a similar experience of taking a wasteland and bringing it to life? How did it make you feel? Were there any surprises along the way?

12. In "Pelican Lessons," Mary writes of ignoring her first instincts while standing in the marsh, watching a trio of enormous white birds descend, and the eventual discovery that "logic" had proved wrong and her gut feelings about what she saw were right the first time. Can you think back to something similar in your own life? Is there a single experience that has tipped the balance for you in terms of trusting your instincts in the future?

13. In "Tool Time," Mary pivots between celebrating her growing independence in handling household problems after her divorce, and mourning the fact that independence can sometimes feel a lot like loneliness. What would you have told her as she sat at the kitchen table and wept that day? Have you ever had to balance a wish or a need to change as a person with caution as to how it would affect the relationship that you are or were in? What did you ultimately do?

14. In "Angels in the Snow," Mary describes the accident that landed her and her daughter in the home of total strangers in the middle of a blizzard. She describes the married couple that took them in as "angels." Have you felt the presence of angels in your life? When and how?

15. Is there a lesson to be taken away from this author's life? What do you think it is, and why do you think it's important?

Made in the USA
Charleston, SC
12 July 2015